The Sixth String of Vilayat Khan

NAMITA DEVIDAYAL

First published in hardback by Context, an imprint of Westland Publications Private Limited, in 2018

Published in paperback by Context, an imprint of Westland Books, a division of Nasadiya Technologies Private Limited, in 2023

No. 269/2B, First Floor, 'Irai Arul', Vimalraj Street, Nethaji Nagar, Alapakkam Main Road, Maduravoyal, Chennai 600095

Westland, the Westland logo, Context and the Context logo are the trademarks of Nasadiya Technologies Private Limited, or its affiliates.

ISBN: 9789357763271

10 9 8 7 6 5 4 3

The views and opinions expressed in this work are the author's own and the facts are as reported by her, and the publisher is in no way liable for the same.

Typeset by SÜRYA, New Delhi

Printed at Saurabh Printers Pvt. Ltd

The Sixth String of Vilayat Khan

Namita Devidayal is the author of *The Music Room* and *Aftertaste*. She is a journalist with *The Times of India*. She lives in Mumbai.

Praise for the book

'The book has his éclat. It is Ustad Vilayat Khan—supremely confident of itself, bold to the point of being brash, totally in awe of the Ustad's genius and yet completely underwhelmed by his obsessive self-absorption.'

– Gopalkrishna Gandhi, *Scroll.in*

'The weighty world of Indian classical music, inhabited by its brilliant practitioners is rendered to the reader in a light-hearted touch and therein lies its appeal.'

– *The Hindu*

'Devidayal's book, based on her interest in the subject and research on the life, time and music of the maestro, provides a wholesome account of the Vilayat Khan phenomenon. Written with sympathy and elegance, this work in fifteen chapters, seeks to capture the personality of the sitarist and his art in all its complexities.'

– *The Book Review*

'Devidayal's acute understanding of classical music and her novelist's eye combine to tell the story of Vilayat Khan in an unconventional narrative that achieves far more than a conventional biography might have, especially in reaching out to a non-specialised readership.'

– *Open*

'Told with a heft but without the heavy hand of a classical music biography, it navigates a genre that bravely blurs the borders between fiction and non-fiction; a leitmotif that runs through both her previous books. It is a bit like the "biographical novel".'

– *The Wire*

'If you pick up *The Sixth String of Vilayat Khan*, read it quietly, taking time off from the demands of daily life, so that you can immerse yourself in the mood of the story as it draws a series of portraits of the sitar maestro.'

– *The Hindu BusinessLine*

'The key that unlocks the deepest truths about Vilayat Khan's life lies in his music, about which Devidayal writes evocatively and with fine insight, giving us a more intimate portrait of the artist than anecdotes can.'

– *Mint*

'As we read, we find ourselves drawn into this world, wanting to belong, even if only by listening to the music. Read it, therefore, with a background of the master himself playing the instrument that was his life.'

– *The New Indian Express*

'There are a lot of anecdotes in the book which were not commonly known and one has to appreciate the author's painstaking research. The book beautifully captures the complicated person Khan was in a respectful and balanced manner.'

– *The Times of India*

'Devidayal, the biographer, is very good at ferreting out facts about the hazy early years of apprenticeship ... Driven by Devidayal's smart prose, the narrative combines fact with fiction.'

– *India Today*

Dedicated to all music lovers

Contents

Shimla
Bhaini Sahib,
Ludhiana
Clement Town, Dehradun
Saharanpur
Delhi
Etawah
Lucknow
Banaras
Gowripur
Indore
Bombay

The Players

Imdad Khan

Enayat Khan *m* Basheeran

- NASEERAN
  m Mohammed Khan — Rais Khan
- ZEENAT
  m Amir Khan — Fehmida
  m Mohammed Shafi
- VILAYAT KHAN
  m Monisha — Shujaat, Yaman, Zila
  m Lisa (Zubeida) — Hidayat
- RAEESAN
  m H.A. Rahi
- IMRAT KHAN
  m Dulhan (Mumtaz) — Sabiha, Nishat, Irshad, Wajahat, Shafaat
  m Belinda — Azmat Ali

Wahid Khan

- KHAN MASTANA
- AZIZ KHAN — Shahid Pervez

This family chart is not complete. It includes only those who feature in the book.

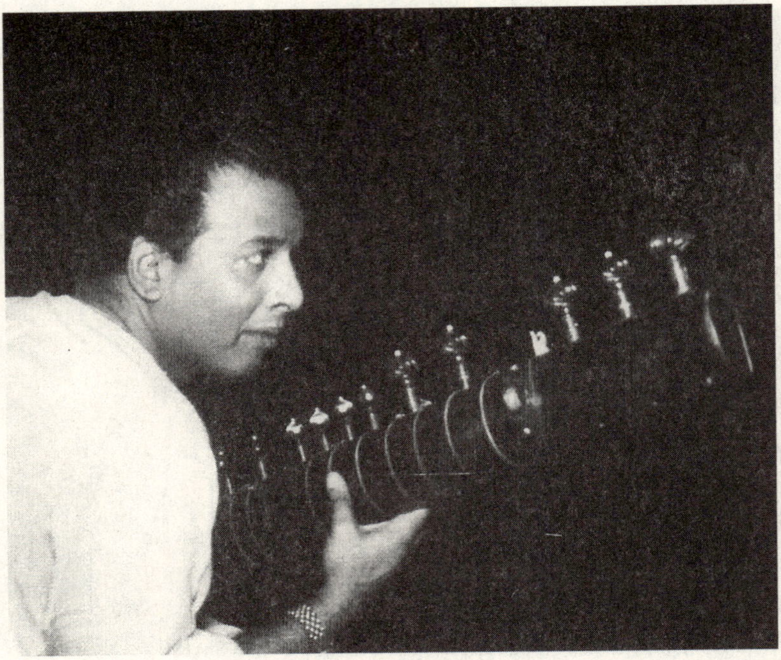

CHAPTER ZERO

Who Is This Vilayat Khan?

1952, Delhi. It had been five years since Independence and India was still in the mood for celebration. Two young string musicians were performing together at the Constitution Club grounds—a sitar player called Ravi Shankar and a sarod player whose name was Ali Akbar Khan. Both were in their early thirties and students of Baba Allauddin Khan, an ambidextrous musician with a goatee, famous for his genius and his temper.

The concert was part of the Jhankar Festival. There was tremendous anticipation around this particular performance and the music fraternity had been buzzing for days. Ravi Shankar had already astonished the world by creating an orchestra for the new All India Radio. Ali Akbar, who happened to be baba's son, was emerging as one of the most refined musicians of his generation. Accompanying them that evening were two tabla masters from Banaras, Kanthe Maharaj and his nephew Kishan.

A covered stage had been constructed on the grounds. The musicians walked up, one behind the other, all wearing white. While they were tuning their instruments, a young man in a black kurta and rimless glasses suddenly appeared in front of the stage, clutching his sitar.

He addressed the audience in beautiful Urdu. 'This stage has so many gorgeous flowers. I would like to add my fragrance by joining my friends Robu-da and Alu-da this evening.'

A murmur of surprise went around the audience. The performance was meant to be a duet. Who was this? Although he spoke poetically, this man had the air of a human detonator. He held his instrument as if it were a weapon, pointing it at phantom enemies. His eyes blazed behind the glasses he wore.

Some recognised him as Vilayat Hussain Khan, the son of Enayat Hussain Khan. A few people started cheering. Baba Allauddin Khan gestured angrily from the front row, trying to stop the duo from becoming a trio, but by then the audience had already expressed its excitement over the intervention and it was too late. The young man jumped onto the stage and the other musicians made space for him.

Baba walked up to the stage and growled at all three: 'Remember, you are all my children. Play with love and respect.'

It was a formidable stage. Ali Akbar sat in the centre, looking vaguely daunted. On either side of him sat the two sitar players, both strikingly good-looking men with large foreheads suggesting grand destinies. Kanthe Maharaj was on one side of the stage. Kishan Maharaj sat on the other side, kneeling in his distinctive manner, as if he were doing namaz. Two grand Miraj tanpuras at the back and two Chicago Radio mikes in front—it was a picture of perfect melodic symmetry.

In the front row sat the undisputed heads of the music world and Delhi's wealthiest patrons, including the Shriram–Shankarlal family. The men were dressed in stylish achkans or suits, the women in gorgeous Banarasi silk saris. They rustled. They coughed. The master of ceremonies introduced the musicians.

Ravi Shankar made the customary gesture asking for permission to begin. He then struck the notes of raga Manj Khamaj. He played for a few minutes then turned to Vilayat Khan, giving him the cue. The younger musician played the same riff, but in a more lilting style. They meandered through the alaap for almost an hour, building gradually, thoughtfully, teasing the ma, the raga's dominant note, the 'manj' in the Khamaj.

At some point, it became evident to the audience that a subtle musical duel was taking place. By the time the faster taans started, the notes had become sharp arrows shot with the intention to annihilate. Ali Akbar Khan hardly got to play, so after a while he quietly put his sarod down and looked bewildered. His head turned from left to right and right to left as the sharpshooters on either side battled on.

At one point, Ravi Shankar hit a set of high notes in the third octave. Like a kite catching its prey, Vilayat Khan scooped up the lid of his little metal oil box and, instead of using his fingers, pressed it on the strings of his instrument. The sound that emerged, of amplified metal on metal, was audacious and amazing. Suddenly, Hafiz Ali Khan got up from his seat and applauded. '*Maar daala!*' He killed him! Others sitting next to him cheered. Baba Alauddin Khan also jumped up and started shouting. 'You have defamed my boys, shuorer baccha, you son of a pig, you scoundrel,' followed by even choicier expletives in Bengali.

The music stopped abruptly.

Twenty-four-year-old Vilayat Khan was declared the winner in the battle of the sitars. He had clearly taken liberties with the music, and even gone a little beyond the parameters of the raga, but he had created an impact. Ravi Shankar did not look pleased. This brash and brilliant musician, seven years younger than him, had humiliated him in public. He quietly got up and left the stage.

The epic concert was discussed by Delhi's music world for days afterwards. Who was this Vilayat Khan, the long-lost son of Enayat? Some weeks later, Ravi Shankar invited Vilayat Khan and Ali Akbar to the radio station to listen to his new orchestra, Vadya Vrinda. They complimented him for integrating elements of Western harmony into Indian music. Afterwards, they all sat in his cabin and had tea with fresh samosas.

Ravi Shankar said, 'Vilayatbhai, this should never happen again.'

Vilayat replied, 'I agree, Robu-da.'

The two musicians promised each other they would never perform together. Kishan Maharaj later told someone, 'If these two eyes of India play together again, one will shut for ever.'

In some ways, the concert may have changed their lives. These two artistes established the sitar as the most popular instrument in India, but their approach to music took two very different directions. Ravi Shankar became a brilliant collaborative artiste who played with the Beatles, Yehudi Menuhin and many others. He was the international star. Vilayat Khan did not achieve the same rock star status, but his music was revolutionary. He transformed the acoustics of the sitar, coaxing it to sing like the human voice.

Ravi Shankar's fame cast a shadow on Vilayat Khan's life, it is hard to deny, but he held on to his aesthetic certainties and stayed true to his music. He consciously avoided what he viewed as titillating populism. Over the next fifty years, Khansahib carefully crafted his personality and his music to become one of the most remarkable creative expressors of the twentieth century.

There are several versions of this story, but they all end in the same epic climax. I discovered very quickly that writing about Vilayat Khan is a bit like chasing a hologram. Everyone has a different memory of him, a different take on the story. He was himself known to be a liberal embellisher of tales. Someone close to him once said: '*Woh toh galti se sach bolte hain.*' He speaks the truth by mistake. His life was iridescent with illusion, which may well have been what he needed to create beyond the ordinary.

Therefore, rather than obsess about factual accuracy, I have tried to create an impressionistic fluid portrait—of a magnificent artiste and a fragmented human being. I have tried to imagine him and tell a story anchored in fact, but narrated with poetic licence, like improvising on a jazz standard. It would be a mistake to regard this strictly as a biography because I am not a historian, but a lover of music and a storyteller. So this is my journey into his life through long discussions with people who were close to him or his family, and also through interviews, archival records and photographs. I have spent many hours listening to his music in solitude. Sometimes, even when the music stops, it continues in my head, and I can see the fairies dancing with sparkles around them, or elephants walking majestically. He used to see his music.

I visited the places where he stayed over the years—Calcutta, Delhi, Bombay, Shimla, Dehradun, and eventually Princeton, in America. I tried to locate him in both place and period, for this is also the story of how music travelled through the ages, and the backdrops changed with broadcasting technologies, changing patronage and Western appreciation.

Ravi Shankar *Ali Akbar Khan* *Vilayat Khan*

Along the way, I met a cast of fabulous characters—musicians and more—who played key notes in his life. I discovered with some wonder that his life has had some curious interconnections with mine: for instance, the iconic 1952 Jhankar concert was organised by the Shriram–Shankarlals who were my great grandfathers; or, Vilayat Khan spent the last decade of his life in Princeton, where I also lived as an undergraduate. But nothing in life is random. Vilayat Khan once told a student who was practising a piece of music at exactly the same time that Khansahib happened to be playing it in another place, 'The music was circulating in the sky when both of us caught it.'

I met Vilayat Khan just once, in Bombay, a year before he died, when he was an older version of the good-looking man I had seen on my parents' HMV record sleeve.

He was staying with his student Arvind Parikh on the quietly posh Altamont Road. The centrepiece in the home was the music room, a space where instruments lined the walls and there was, instead of the clutter of furniture, a vast carpet on which there were always musicians and students, strumming and singing and gossipping, or discussing the many approaches to a particular raga.

It is here that I met him. A mini-durbar was in session, with Khansahib's sitar resting before him and his wife Lisa and some students scattered around, an audience in perpetuity. He was framed against a Pichwai dotted with gilded cows. He wore a silvery grey silk kurta. A thick gold chain with the Islamic triple talisman sat around his neck, a large solitaire sparkled on his finger. His hair was grey, his teeth stained, but he was still enormously attractive. He spoke in a slow deliberate baritone while meticulously crafting a paan with ingredients from a little silver box.

My chubby one-year-old son fearlessly crawled up to him.

Khansahib picked him up, put him on his lap, hugged him tight and said, '*Khuda khush rakhe.*' May he be blessed. He gave the boy his rosary beads to play with. Khansahib had a fractured relationship with his own grandchildren because of deep and painful rifts in the family.

I had grown up listening to stories about his stormy, wondrous life—that he was a better musician than Ravi Shankar; that he loved ballroom dancing and cars and women; he made outstanding partridge curry; he always needed to win, even if it meant cheating at the card game … even if it meant hurting those closest to him. So I was a bit overwhelmed. But for those few minutes, I met a kind and loving man.

My journey into his life is also an attempt to understand that abiding paradox: how anarchy can coexist with harmony. How pain can be an underlying constant in life but can also be converted into beauty. What I discovered along the way is that the life of a genius is not easy, nor harmonious.

He was mad and divine, filled with contradiction, mercurial, selfish, sometimes even hateful, and other times filled with the most overwhelming expressions of love. In the end, his music transcends all else. And it makes the listener want to embrace him—and the world.

This is the love story of Vilayat Khan and his music.

CHAPTER ONE

The Early Years

His first memory of music: the colour yellow. No words. Only sound, sublime. Albert Hall in Calcutta. He was six years old. His father walked onto the stage carrying a sitar, ringlets cascading down either side of his neck, and everyone stood up, even the British governor. The music began, like a giant wave in slow motion, gradually pulling everyone in. Then the picture grew blurry. The child kept falling asleep and waking up, floating between dream and reality, the two spaces linked only by sound. His eyes suddenly opened to loud claps. That's when he saw a haze of yellow all around.

'Arre, Vilayat miyan,' his father said playfully the next morning. 'My silly, sweet child! That was the colour of Basant, of spring. You saw the raga.'

In the old days, great artistes believed that their children should learn music before they learned how to speak or read and write. Without the clutter of words, the child absorbs music like a sponge. That is how music becomes his first language. It establishes itself as an interiority that will influence everything he later does and feels. It creates a direct connection to the universe because unstruck music lives in rivers and birdsong and in silence.

Vilayat Khan was not yet ten when his father Enayat Khan died. But the fire had been lit. The father had carried his little miyan into that parallel world where sound translates into colour, where memory triggers composition. There was no going back. Besides, music flowed in the boy's bloodstream. He was born into the greatest sitar gharana—the son of Enayat Khan and the grandson of Imdad Khan.

Dada Imdad Khan was originally from Etawah, near Lucknow, in north India. He served as a court musician in the state of Indore for many years. Imdad Khan found his way to Calcutta around the turn of the century, to a city that was turning into a great centre of music, especially instrumental music. One of the reasons for this could be that, some years before the Revolt of 1857, Wajid Ali Shah, the nawab of Oudh, who had spent less time ruling and more time playing his sitar, was exiled by the British to Metiabruz just outside Calcutta. A massive entourage of court musicians followed him there, like creatures behind the Pied Piper, not entirely sure where they were headed. Perhaps because Wajid Ali himself favoured the sitar, instrumental players gravitated to Calcutta, while vocal musicians found their way to that other emerging commercial centre, Bombay.

This was the time when the princely states were being replaced by mercantile cities like Calcutta and Bombay. The merchant sahibs became the new maharajas, and an aspirational imperative made them want to take over the rather posh job of patronising the arts, just like their royal predecessors. Performing artistes were the beneficiaries of this impulse.

In Calcutta, this English-educated Indian upper class was also looking for ways to rediscover and reimagine its identity. There was a growing ambivalence towards British customs and impositions—while on the one hand they wanted to fit in with the sahibs, on the other they felt a need to reassert their sense of Indianness.

Imdad Khan was invited to Calcutta by two wealthy brothers, Jatindra Mohan and Sourindra Mohan Tagore, distant relatives of Rabindranath Tagore, who were art lovers, philanthropists and students of the sitar. Sometime in the late 1800s, the younger brother, Sourindra Mohan, had even established two music colleges—the Bangla Sangeet Vidyalaya and the Bengal Academy of Music—to restore the respectability of Indian music among Bengal's elite. Thanks to the Tagores and later another wealthy babu, Tara Prasad Ghosh, Imdad Khan lived on and off in Bengal for almost twenty-five years, spending the latter half in Ghosh's home on Beadon Street in north Calcutta.

But performing artistes in those days were like gypsy kings. Even the greatest musicians had to move around from court to court and find the best job, the best deal. Imdad Khan was fond of travel, and took his sons Enayat and Wahid all over on the new railway network that had just been established across the country. He became a truly national star, regarded equally for sitar and surbahar, the bass sitar. He came to Bombay's newly formed performance mandalis and made it as far south as Mysore. In the process, he ensured that his two boys got access to the best musicians and even bits of training under them. He was one of the first instrumental musicians to be recorded by the British-owned Gramophone & Typewriter Company of India, after which he became popular across India. There were marvellous legends around him. He was once said to have soothed a rogue elephant with his music during a conference in Bagri, Nepal. Other musicians would say, if Dada Imdad Khan is in the audience, you cannot play Puriya or Yaman because he is the established king of those ragas.

Imdad Khan also did something that had not been done before—he taught numerous non-hereditary musicians, including Brajendra Kishore Roy Chowdhury, the raja of Gowripur, a small state in what is now Bangladesh. The sitar gradually metamorphosed into a delightful parlour instrument, copycatting the British custom of chamber performance. Calcutta's feudal aristocracy started hosting sitar performances in the chandeliered living rooms of their palatial homes. It was also a relatively new instrument, and not considered as downmarket as the sarangi, nor as stoic as the veena.

An interesting pedagogical development at the time was the introduction of sitar performance manuals. These booklets were a curious by-product of the English education system and marked a first-time shift in India from oral to written transmission of music. *The Sitar Siksa* by Krishnadhan Bandopadhyaya was even written with Western notations. Thanks to these manuals, the sitar went from being a professional musician's instrument to the amateur's plaything. People from non-musical backgrounds started playing, and it became a regular feature in many homes.

Imdad Khan contributed vastly towards creating this new market for the sitar. His music merged past and future—which musician and chronicler Hans Utter describes as a kind of nostalgia for the Mughal empire with the romance of a modern India. He took out the more old-fashioned dhrupad elements, and brought in vocal khayal and thumri embellishments in keeping with the aesthetic demands of the time.

Imdad Khan eventually returned to Indore and spent most of his last years there. He died in 1920, by which time the sitar had found a new and respectable place among the Calcutta elite.

A year or two after Imdad Khan's death, his son Enayat moved from Indore to Bengal and settled into this welcoming musical landscape. He spent many years in the court of Gowripur, where his father had also served, joining some of the greatest instrumentalists of the time, including Hafiz Ali Khan and Baba Allauddin Khan.

It was in Gowripur that Vilayat Khan was born. His documented birth year is 1928, but some suggest that he was born a couple of years earlier. Soon after, Enayat Khan moved with his family to Calcutta, to a house he named 'Riyaz', in the vibrant Muslim neighbourhood of Park Circus. He lived there for most of the forty-eight years of his life, and some giant moments in Calcutta's musical history took place within the rooms that surrounded its triangular courtyard.

Like his father, Enayat Khan established himself as an incredible sitar and surbahar player at a very young age and used to be called 'Bengal ka Jadugar', the Magician of Bengal. He lived between Calcutta and Gowripur, where he was treated with great regard as a senior court musician by the Roy Chowdhury family. There are stories that describe how he used to ride down the street on a white horse, and women threw open their windows to catch a glimpse of the man with ringlets cascading down either side of his ears, making him look rather like a handsome rabbi.

In 1934, a teenager called Rabindra Shankar Chowdhury, who later changed his name to Ravi Shankar, heard one of Enayat Khan's students, a young man called Amiya Kanti Bhattacharya, play the sitar in Calcutta. He was so impressed by Bhattacharya's finger-work that he resolved to learn from the same teacher. But the night before young Robu was to formalise his relationship with Enayat Khan by having the ceremonial thread tied round his wrist, he got typhoid and had to be hospitalised. The moment was lost and he never went back.

In a strange twist of fate, around the same time, another young boy called Vilayat Khan was being initiated into this great tradition. It happened thus one night. Enayat Khan was sitting around with his usual coterie of fans and students when he called for his son. That afternoon he had got Vilayat's school report card with zeros against almost every subject. Before showing it to his father, the little boy had overwritten the numbers, but in his childish enthusiasm, the total added up to more than a 100 per cent.

'So, Miyan. Do you want to continue going to school or focus on music?'

The little boy looked around nervously and knew that the question was mostly rhetorical.

'Music, Abba.'

'Think about what you are saying. Going to school is easy. This stuff is like eating lohe ke chane, nuts of steel. It is no easy matter.'

'Yes, Abba.'

The young Vilayat left the room but hid behind the door, evesdropping on the conversation between his father and the others. They were admonishing Enayat Khan for being so harsh with his young boy.

'Oh, be quiet all of you. Donkeys and geniuses will never see eye to eye,' he said, slurring heavily, for he had been drinking. 'This boy will one day transform sound into colour and fragrance.'

From the very next day, Vilayat stopped going to school. Enayat Khan started supervising his son's practice, waking him early in the mornings, sometimes kicking him gently. Vilayat's little fingers would swell up, riven with cuts. Before the cuts could heal and callous, he would be told to play some more, and they would start bleeding again. Gradually, his fingers became hard like lead. And gradually, a musician was born.

About a year later, one of Enayat Khan's students, Bhupen Ghosh, organised the All-Bengal Music Conference at Madan Theatre and suggested that the eight-year-old Vilayat should start the programme.

Very reluctantly, after a lot of persuasion, Enayat Khan agreed, though he firmly believed that children should not be applauded before their time. An otherwise fearless man was besieged with nervousness about his son's debut performance. News about the programme had created a stir in the city. The audience was filled with some of the greatest musicians of the time; they had all come to listen to Enayat's young lad.

While he was waiting in the wings, the great tabaliya Ahmed Jan Thirakwa said to Enayat Khan, 'Don't worry! I will accompany the boy in such a way that he will sound perfect.'

He winked at little Vilayat. 'In fact, he will handle me!'

Vilayat went on stage and, without much ado, played raga Bhairavi. For the next few days, all he heard was praise and blessings and grand speculation about his future.

Soon after that, the Megaphone Recording Company produced a 78 rpm in which the father played on one side and the prodigy son played on the other, ragas Bhairavi and Miyan ki Todi. Times were good, the applause rolled in, and Enayat Khan took his son wherever he went.

But the joy was shortlived. Like many great artistes, Enayat Khan lived with that sweet and dangerous delusion that because his art had touched immortality, his life would as well. He was a reckless alcoholic. He had grown dependent on the choicest imported whiskies and brandies which were available to him in the princely courts. He didn't pay attention to his doctor's increasingly dire warnings that he needed to stop drinking immediately.

Enayat Khan was at the Prayag Music Conference in Allahabad in November 1938 where he continued drinking, vomited blood and fainted. The ten-year-old Vilayat was with him. He was terrified, even though this had happened once before. While he was sobbing and dabbing his father's face with a damp cloth, someone said to him, 'You should save your father's honour and play the sitar in his place.'

The concert was slotted for four in the afternoon, but Vilayat played a short energetic morning Bhairavi, for that was all he knew well.

Enayat Khan was taken back to Calcutta. The train journey was difficult, but he made it home, barely conscious. Later that night, he lay resting, breathing with great difficulty, while his wife Basheeran Begum sat by his side fanning him. Vilayat woke up around midnight to the sound of his mother wailing.

The death of a father can have a catastrophic impact on any family, but in this case, it may have been the single most important catalyst in the musical legacy that Vilayat Khan would go on to create.

The lives of great artistes often reveal that their destiny has been influenced by unseen forces and unlikely people. It is possible that Vilayat Khan's music may have been quite different had Enayat Khan lived longer.

After Enayat's death, the house in Park Circus was no longer the same. Where there had been only music and applause, there now was a roar of silence. The cutglass decanters gifted by his wealthy friends no longer sparkled. A film of dust settled on the sitar and it dissipated into a state of chronic tunelessness.

The young Vilayat started feeling more and more hopeless. All the wealthy patrons, fawning students and endless hangers-on who used to gather in their home when Enayat Khan was alive, evaporated like the Hooghly mist. In their place was a young mother whose moods swung between grief and anger, a baby brother, sisters of various ages and a growing sense of imminent penury. Quite apart from the material peril, there was that deeper, incoherent gloom that a child could sense.

Basheeran Begum, or Amma, was a little over thirty and scarcely able to handle herself. When she was not sobbing, she prayed, vigorously and loudly, almost as if she were berating her benefactor. She started wearing the purdah again—a practice her husband had stopped her from following when he was alive. Basheeran Begum was breathtakingly beautiful, with pale translucent skin and almond eyes, as if she had stepped out of a miniature painting.

The children scuttled around Amma like little squirrels in the house, watching her with dismay, hiding if she was in one of her moods. Vilayat had to retune himself from being the adored boy into a little man. But instead of trying to comfort Vilayat, Amma would often fly into fits of random rage.

'Practice! Practice! Who do you think is going to support the family now? Are you going to cut grass or are you going to become a musician?' she screeched, holding the baby Raeesan at her waist. 'Where are all your father's acolytes when we need them? Everyone is a fair-weather friend here. Not like my people in Saharanpur. They are sincere, godfearing people. Allah miyan, what are we going to do?'

She roused Vilayat early in the mornings to get him to do his riyaz, peeling off the blanket so that the cold would wake him up instantly. There are stories that she would even give him a mild electric shock from the lamp to wake him. Sometimes, she would cajole him by playing cards with him.

And every so often, he would sit alone with his sitar, facing the wall, under a portrait of his grandfather. The boy, still young enough to be wearing half-pants, would play the kind of music that would make the grand old man in the picture smile. His music rose from the immediate physical space into one where the seen meets the unseen. In those moments, his mother stood at the door, tears rolling down her cheeks as she sent him silent blessings.

But after a while, the boy just stopped playing his sitar. He stopped going out to play with friends as well. His world seemed to have come to an end. No one said anything and even his mother seemed to have lost the stamina to push.

It may have been about six months into this silent dirge that Vilayat was dejectedly browsing through an old album of photographs that lay inside his father's cupboard. It contained pictures of his handsome father as a young man. His grandfather, looking regal in a turban. His uncles were all around, holding their instruments with pride. Then he saw it—the black-and-white picture of a little boy in a white silk shirt on stage…

He couldn't forget that day. The headiness of that moment kept coming back with amplified clarity. The memory of those hours of practice with his father's alternately gentle and rough goading haunted him. Vilayat desperately wanted that same feeling again. He couldn't believe that all this had been so cruelly snatched from him.

He remembered the times when his father would make him

play or just listen, for listening was as big a part of learning. The young boy would sit amidst the people who came to visit, and fall asleep on his father's lap while listening to stories about all the great musicians of the past.

One story in particular came to him recurrently and vividly in his dreams. It was about his grandfather, Dada Imdad Khan. He was known as the four-candle man, because in the days before clocks, he would light four candles one after another and practice for as long as they burned. During one such session, when one of the candles was halfway down, a relative burst into his room and said that Imdad Khan's daughter was very ill and he needed to see her immediately. Dada replied that his candle was still burning, so he couldn't leave yet. With the next candle, the same thing happened. Midway into the third candle, the girl died. Imdad Khan never forgave himself for being remiss as a father, but his ruthless commitment to music remained unchanged. It is said that he had done the famous forty-day chilla, a rigorous and exhaustive ritual where the musician doesn't leave the house for forty days and only practices music.

It was this kind of legacy that Vilayat Khan was born into and breathed in. He knew he had to do something, but he wasn't quite sure what. Over the next couple of years, the teenaged Vilayat was consumed by a restless energy that would become his abiding companion.

I went back into the labyrinthine heart of old Calcutta, and found my way to the house in Park Circus on a road that had been renamed Enayat Khan Avenue. I was looking for something, a moment in history, a sound of music.

The house was locked. Vilayat Khan is dead. His children

too are scattered across the world. Shujaat lives in Delhi, Hidayat is based in Princeton and Zila is in Bombay. Yaman is no more. Vilayat Khan's brother Imrat has been living in St Louis, Missouri with an American wife. The siblings and cousins barely speak to one another.

A little distance away from the house, next to the Pavlov Hospital for the mentally ill, is the Gobra Muslim Cemetery. This vast unkempt ground is the resting place of some of India's greatest musicians. I walked into it one blazing afternoon.

Here lay the grave of Enayat Khan, Bengal ka Jadugar. The elaborate tombstone fashioned to look like a medieval monument was chipped, but as a ruin it was, if anything, more heartbreakingly beautiful. A few feet away, under an ancient banyan, lay the remains of Karamatullah Khan, the great tabla player. On the far side of the burial ground was the grave of Amir Khan, the majestic singer, Vilayat Khan's friend and mentor whose life was prematurely extinguished by an alcohol-fuelled car crash in Calcutta.

And, at the feet of his father, several feet below an indifferent cement slab, lay Vilayat Khan. A spider's web ran across it like a sacred thread.

Grass overwhelmed most of the tombstones. Long-dried garlands of tube roses suggested that it had been a while since someone murmured prayers here. I asked the cemetery-keeper whether anyone came to pay their respects to these national treasures, recalling the way tourists flock to Jim Morrison's tomb in Paris. He shook his head and asked for baksheesh if I hoped to get any further information from him. Walking around, I saw a few undead men smoking their peace pipes in the shadows of the graves.

The silence of this timeless place was broken by the distant whistle of a train. Perhaps life had become so unmanageable for the living that they didn't have time for the dead, even if those buried had once brought heaven and earth together.

'No matter where I die, I wish to be placed at the feet of abba,' Vilayat Khan had told one of his friends some years before his death, after kneeling at his father's grave. 'Right here, in Calcutta. Please ensure it.'

Vilayat Khan ran away to every corner of India and the world throughout his life, but Calcutta remained the constant in his heart. The place haunted his imagination like a boatman's song. Wherever he was, by November, he would be back there like a homing pigeon, and stay till February. He slipped into Bengali like it was his mother tongue. He loved his mustard fish, his walks along the Hooghly, and the first call to prayer which brought raga Bilaskhani Todi floating in through his window like a morning bird. It was one of the few things in his life that centred him, realigned him with himself, for otherwise Khansahib belonged to a universe that was not rooted in geography.

MADE IN INDIA
Columbia
This patented copyright record must not be publicly performed without licence
Hindi Song
BEX. 257
Sung by—LATE
K. S. ABDUL KARIM KHAN
COLUMBIA GRAPHOPHONE CO. LTD.

MEGAPHONE
REGISTERED
TRADE MARK
INSTRUMENTAL
SUR BAHAR
M.C.C. 25
Prof. Enayet Khan
OE 1525
MADE IN INDIA

REGD. TRADE MARK OF
THE GRAMOPHONE CO., LTD.
HIS MASTER'S VOICE
SIDE ONE
HINDUSTANI
CLASSICAL
EALP. 1292
TARPAT HUN JAISE-Lalit
UNGANG LAGI ANKHIA (Comp. Self)-Ramkeli
GARWA MAIN SANG LAGE-Todi
ARI MERO NAHI-Desi Dhamar-Hori
BAJU BAND KHUL KHUL JAYE-Thumri Bhairavi
MORE JOBANOA PAR AAI-Dadra
USTAD FAIYAZ KHAN SAHIB
EMI
MADE IN INDIA

REGD. TRADE MARK OF
THE GRAMOPHONE CO., LTD.
HIS MASTER'S VOICE
STEREO
INSTRUMENTAL
CLASSICAL
Side One
ECSD. 2772
SITAR :
RAGA : ALHAIYA BILAWAL
GAT : TRITAAL
USTAD VILAYAT KHAN
EMI
MADE IN INDIA

CHAPTER TWO

The Making of a Musician

The real force behind the teenaged Vilayat was a determined and ambitious woman—Basheeran Begum. Like many daughters and wives from musical families, she had learned by osmosis, just as women from business families understood the inner workings of money by listening to a lifetime of conversations between fathers, uncles, brothers and sons. It was in their blood. But there was no question of these women ever performing or teaching, for that was a space occupied by the courtesan. They would tend to a husband or son while he practised late into the night, fanning him, bringing him food, imbibing everything musically, but remaining the silent partner.

Realising that her son was prodigiously gifted, Basheeran Begum took it upon herself to ensure that his musical training continued with the vigour required to get him to the level of proficiency that had made his forefathers famous. She taught him how to think about the raga, its pace, its character. Blind practice is not enough, she said, especially when you begin to mature as a musician.

It is said that she also went to her sister's husband and

begged him to do something unheard of in those times—to teach her, a woman, certain ragas so that she could in turn teach and guide her son. 'I am forgoing my hijab, my modesty, and you must help me,' she said.

It is entirely possible that Basheeran Begum viewed her elder son as a potential breadwinner who would alleviate some of the catastrophic poverty that had enveloped the family. Their deprivation was, perhaps, felt more keenly because the family had lived so well when Enayat Khan was alive. Her consistent efforts with her son—who shared a great physical likeness to her—veered between aggressive and desperate, all of which gradually took a toll on their relationship.

On a bitingly cold winter's day, one of Enayat Khan's old students, a relative of the Gowripur raja, dropped in at the Park Circus house. He greeted Basheeran Begum and looked around the room where he used to have his lessons.

'How are you, Miyan?' he asked, addressing the young Vilayat the way his father used to. 'I can see you are now sprouting a bit of a moustache. Wah wah!'

'Kaku, will you please teach me the second half of the Chhaya Nat composition?' asked Vilayat shyly. 'Abba only taught me the sthayi, the first section.'

'Ha ha, the little Khansahib wants to learn, eh? Well, to get it out of your father, I had to go through all kinds of loops. I had to wait. I had to lavish money on him. It didn't just come my way. Now it's your turn to pay your dues. Why don't you start pressing my legs if you want anything from me. Then we can tie the ceremonial ganda and make you my official disciple.'

Vilayat ran into his mother's room and started boxing his

pillow furiously. His sister Zeenat looked on, tears in her eyes, then hugged him wordlessly.

That was a turning point in his life. Vilayat realised that there was very little left for him in Calcutta. He had to get out. And he would return only once he had become a star.

Even at that age, he had an ambition fuelled by a rage over which he had little control. It became his signature, a recurring feature in his life—anger that would erupt randomly, sometimes unwarrantedly, when things didn't go his way. It is said that, as a young man, Vilayat Khan once went to a learned musician in Indore to memorise a composition that only that man knew. The musician was reluctant, though. Vilayat initially tried to woo him by pressing his feet, but it didn't work; he then brought him opium, thinking that that might do the trick; he went back and returned with some cash, but even that didn't work. Finally, Vilayat reached into his pocket, pulled out a pistol, held it to the musician's head and said, 'Will you teach me, or do you wish to die?' He extracted what he wanted.

Humiliation—especially when it strikes an impressionable teenager—can catalyse either self-destruction or single-minded ambition. Vilayat Khan was destined to defy mediocrity and a series of events and individuals helped pave his way.

Early one morning, while the crescent moon was still up and everyone slept, the young Vilayat slipped out of the house with a few rupees and a sitar. He would have been about fourteen, though there is no documented evidence of his age. He had no idea where he was headed, but made his way to Howrah station and hopped ticketless on to a train bound for Delhi.

Vilayat Khan's journey from Calcutta to Delhi was both the most difficult and most important journey of his life. The stories surrounding his running away have become legendary and embellished over the years and retellings. He boarded various trains, somewhat aimlessly, but he vaguely knew he wanted to get to Delhi. Some ticket collectors took pity on him, others treated him like an urchin and ordered him off the train. He spent one night in a small, unknown railway station, lying curled up on a cold bench, clutching his instrument, and suddenly missed his mother and the other children. He had a dream about her standing at the door, with baby Imrat at her waist, holding a glass of hot milk for him.

But this was Vilayat Khan. He got on another train and finally reached Old Delhi station. Here, he spent a few hours aimlessly wandering along the banks of the Yamuna. It is unclear exactly how he found his way there but, somehow, he made it to Broadcasting House, the building that housed the recently established All India Radio, or AIR.

The guard at the door refused to let him in, but Vilayat was unrelenting. When he finally managed to enter, Vilayat collapsed at the feet of AIR's distinguished programme director Zulfiqar Ali Bukhari, who had moved from Lahore to head this new broadcasting force. Bukhari saw the dishevelled boy with a sitar and stared hard.

'Are you who I think you are? Enayat ka beta? Vilayat?'

'Yes. I am informing you that I have run away from home, and if you attempt to send me back, I will run away from here as well.'

Bukhari was a great lover of music and a longstanding fan of Enayat Khan's. He had also heard the record in which the father and son had played together. Moved by powerful empathy for this boy, Bukhari knew that he had to give Vilayat Khan shelter from the storm.

'Don't worry, son. Come with me. You can stay here and do some work in the studio.'

Bukhari virtually adopted the young Vilayat, allowing him to live in the tin-roofed garage next to the radio canteen, practise his music in a room at the station, and also to sit in on long recording sessions by some of the greatest artistes of that time. He was given odd jobs like cleaning and tuning the tanpuras. Bukhari guided him with tender affection, and instructed the canteen staff to give Vilayat food only after he had finished his daily practice.

The radio station became one of the surrogate teachers that the teenaged Vilayat would adopt over the next few years. His other teachers were a clutch of musicians—some of whom were dead but could still be heard through the crackling mechanism of the gramophone.

In fact, two technological revolutions of the early twentieth century in India had a significant impact on Vilayat Khan's formative years—the gramophone and radio.

Until then, musical communication was so primitive that a listener in Lucknow may never have got to hear a Carnatic musician from Mysore. But these technologies changed the way music was transmitted and taught. With records proliferating the marketplace, there was a new musical democracy, and anyone from the aspiring amateur to the ambitious artiste could place a needle on the round disc, listen to the greatest names of the time and imitate them or copy their style. Music thus broke free of the cloistered confines of hereditary musicians who had guarded their knowledge obsessively, taught students selectively and remained permanently suspicious of outsiders. To start with, some musicians were frightened of the recording devices, and one famously thought that if he sang into the big gramophone it would steal his voice.

The Gramophone & Typewriter Company of India, which later became His Master's Voice, was the main force in the recording industry and was based in Calcutta. By 1908, the demand for published records was so high that the company opened a record-pressing factory in Sealdah and later Dum Dum, both suburbs of Calcutta. It recorded vigorously and popularised all kinds of music—classical vocal, light, instrumental—taking these genres out of private living rooms into the public domain. For three rupees, anyone could buy a record and listen to these 'singers and songstresses' as they were called. Soon, numerous small recording companies sprouted across the country, including Dwarkin & Son and Universal Record in Calcutta, and Beka Record Company and Ramagraph Record in Bombay.

As a young boy with no father or teacher to guide him, Vilayat Khan became obsessed with listening to the 78 rpm records of past musicians, especially vocalists. He spent hours listening to Abdul Karim Khan, Abdul Wahid Khan, Faiyaz Khan, Zohrabai Agrewali and later Kesarbai Kerkar. He learned their music by heart, each note and phrase and pause. Though he had no formal education, he had a photographic aural memory and his mental spools were constantly active. The musicologist Deepak Raja, who has analysed Vilayat Khan's music extensively, suggests that this extraordinary quality revealed itself in his music throughout his life; echoes and references from past masters brought to his playing a haunting quality that left the audience mesmerised, touched by a feeling of déjà vu, even if they didn't quite know why.

While the recording industry catered to a more elite clientele which could afford the 'talking machines' or gramophone players, it was the radio that became an even bigger force in nurturing and spreading classical music in the newly independent India.

All India Radio was launched in 1936, a few years before Vilayat Khan reached Bukhari's doorstep. Before that, the first radio stations in India were the Radio Club of Bombay and the Calcutta Radio Club and a few more in some princely states such as Mysore, where Dada Imdad Khan had produced his first recording. All India Radio was a revolutionary broadcasting force for a new India, and a series of British and Indian officers were assigned the challenging charge of setting it up. Lionel Fielden, an Englishman who put it all together, wrote in his memoir, *A Natural Bent*, that 'none of the staff had ever seen a microphone before and they found great difficulty in using it, or in believing that it was of any use', while most of the radio artistes 'ate opium and refused to come to rehearsal in their "opium time"'.

It was a new world. Musicians, habituated to long performances and vast halls, were wary of the boxy rooms at the station and of microphones stealing their voices. Punctuality was always an issue and they were loathe to abide by the restrictions of time and duration that broadcasting demanded. Station directors had to deftly manoeuvre around their eccentricities.

There is a story about a senior vocalist who arrived at the station wearing a long achkan, a pink turban and purple suede shoes, with a crew of accompanists and disciples in tow. When he was told that his broadcast had to fit into an hour, he roared with outrage and said that he usually took two hours just to warm up and that his concerts were all-night affairs. The station director tried to negotiate with him and offered him an extra hour. The singer refused. At this point, the programming officer whispered something in the station director's ear and they both smiled. He continued negotiating with the artiste, who finally consented to three hours.

When the vocalist sat down to sing at 6 p.m., the clever

programme officer switched on the red broadcast light—but he did not connect the studio to the broadcast circuit. Instead, the station aired its usual half-hour programme for children from the adjoining studio, followed by another half-hour show on better agricultural practices for rural listeners. By then, the singer had done a series of slow movements in raga Shyam Kalyan and warmed up beautifully, blissfully unaware that he was being tricked. At 7 p.m. sharp, the music went on air, flowing into many thousand wireless radios across the country. About five minutes before 9 p.m., the station director gingerly opened the door to the studio and, with a smile, pointed to the clock. The artiste complied by wrapping up his performance with a few fast taans. The show was over and everyone was pleased.

There were also many occasions when radio officials had to placate artistes and tell them that it was not lowbrow to have ordinary people on the streets listen to their music. But gradually, it became evident that radio was the new patron of music and the greatest musicians of the time started flocking to the stations, getting more comfortable with this space and enjoying the wide publicity it gave them. All India Radio became the first major institutional employer of Indian classical musicians.

All India Radio felt comfortable enough in that role to innovate, or ask for interventions that it felt were the need of the hour. In a curious move in 1940, John Foulds, a musician and composer who had been brought in to head the Delhi station's Western music section, proposed that the harmonium be banned on radio as an instrument of accompaniment because it was foreign and could not glide smoothly between notes. His view was widely supported. Even Rabindranath Tagore wrote a letter stating that he had banned the harmonium in Santiniketan for those very reasons.

It was this incredibly charged atmosphere that the young Vilayat Khan dropped into, and here he managed to recreate the magical world that had been lost to him with the death of his father. Soon enough, under the watchful eye of Bukhari, he was encouraged to play for broadcasts from the Delhi station, although for many years radio had been biased towards vocal musicians.

The radio station also gave Vilayat Khan the opportunity to regularly meet and become close to many other fine musicians—such as the percussionist Alla Rakha, and the sarod player Ali Akbar Khan, who was employed at the Lucknow station but travelled regularly to Delhi. This was also where he learned from senior artistes who came to record from all over India. By spending time around them and listening to their work, he picked up numerous compositions and styles.

On most days, by about noon, musicians would gather in the rooms of the station directors and sit around chatting, singing, exchanging compositions. If one was singing, another might say, 'Now listen to the partner composition.' They would critique, they would praise, and they would steal music from each other. The topics of discussion ranged from deconstructing a rare raga to whether the harmonium ban on radio was justified. While senior artistes usually sat with the director, singing and playing, the youngsters stood at the back, paying careful attention and not daring to interrupt.

One afternoon, a well-known singer said, 'Listen to my composition in raga Desh. I created it last night.'

After he was done, another musician said, 'Sahib, forgive me for saying this, but not one phrase in this is your own.'

Everyone was silent at this affront. A respectable musician had just been accused of plagiarism. Vilayat Khan looked at Ali Akbar Khan and winked. The two youngsters were thoroughly enjoying the entertainment.

'What makes you think you have created this?' the musician continued. 'What our seniors have done before you, no one can top or match. Let us be humble that we are only repeating something that was made long before us by people much greater than us.'

Great music and great food always seemed to go together in this world. One or the other of the ustads would bring kababs and parathas for all to share. One day, after Vilayat Khan had been there for almost a year, he mustered up the courage and said to a senior vocalist, 'Khansahib, please can I take ten compositions from you?' The musician laughed and said, 'Why ten? Take hundred, Mashallah. But in return, you have to bring as many keema parathas for us all to share tomorrow.'

During these years, the newly emerging India was confronted with the need to bring together a maddeningly diverse set of cultures, customs and languages. Radio, therefore, was also seen as a propitious medium for the creation of a unified nationalist narrative. It was used to create a standardised time (Indian Standard Time) as well as a common language (English and Hindi), launching an entirely new experience: a national voice.

By 1947, nine broadcasting stations had been established. With Partition, the Delhi, Lucknow, Madras, Trichinopoly, Bombay and Calcutta stations stayed in India, while the Lahore, Peshawar and Dacca stations went to Pakistan. The new Indian government started viewing Indian classical music as a way to create a national culture. It launched the first National Programme of Music in 1952, broadcasting Hindustani and Carnatic music on alternate Saturday evenings. A few years later, it started the Radio Sangeet Sammelan concert-broadcast series, where it sponsored and aired performances across the country to add the 'live' element that is often more flavourful than studio recordings.

Not all the new systems at All India Radio worked in favour of musicians. Following a British cultural custom, the government eventually created a system of grading artistes and slotting them into categories which dictated both their airtime and their fees. This didn't go down well with everyone. Vilayat Khan would eventually become the most outspoken critic of what he considered an unnatural and arbitrary method of judging art and artistes. After 1952, he would refuse to have anything to do with All India Radio.

This formative decade in Vilayat Khan's life remains blurry and many of the stories and places fold into one another, but it is likely that the young teenager moved between Calcutta, Delhi and a dusty town called Saharanpur, his maternal grandparents' home, just north of Delhi. Fatherless and ambitious, Vilayat attached himself to a variety of mentors who became solid rocks in his life, preventing him from drifting into oblivion, which was the fate of so many other musicians' children.

One such person was Dhrubatara Joshi, a man whom Vilayat's father had tutored and loved like a son. Joshi babu was an erudite musician from Lucknow who spoke English and Urdu with the same felicity that he played the sitar and sang. His biological parents were doctors, but Enayat Khan had always referred to him as his first son.

Sometime after Enayat Khan's death, Joshi babu sent a message to Vilayat, 'I have some of your family wealth, so please come and take it from me whenever you are ready.'

Vilayat did. He went and spent time with Joshi babu in Lucknow and later Delhi. Their relationship was most unusual. Vilayat viewed Joshi babu as an elder brother and teacher, but

Joshi looked up to him equally because Vilayat was his guru's son, and therefore the gharana's khalifa or head.

Vilayat must have been in his mid-teens when he arrived one morning at Joshi babu's house in Lucknow carrying only his instrument. He seemed to be in a daze. After a quick salam to everyone, he went straight into the room assigned to him, sat down facing a wall, and started playing a single phrase over and over. The people sitting in the room outside looked at one another in disbelief.

Joshi babu's wife came inside and said, 'Vilayatbhai, at least wash up and have something to eat and drink.'

'No. I practice each palta 1,000 times and I managed to finish 700 before leaving home. Now I have to finish the other 300 before I have my cup of tea.'

Joshi babu silently beckoned to her to leave the young boy alone. He watched Vilayat for a while and then went back into the other room.

'Let him be. He has his grandfather's blood in him. Imdad Khan treated his music like prayer. Just as a devotee rolls out his mat and sits down to pray at a fixed time, he did the same with his practice.' He then told the gathered family members the story of a time when Dada was travelling. When the train stopped at Ratlam station, he quietly stepped out of the compartment, rolled out his rug on the platform floor, and sat down to play, oblivious to everything until the guard went up and nudged him, gently informing him that the whistle had just been blown, so he must get back on the train.

Later that night, Vilayat said to Joshi babu, 'Please listen to this composition I have come up with in raga Darbari.'

He played it and Joshi babu's eyes instantly filled up. He recognised it as Enayat Khan's composition. Vilayat Khan must have heard it played so often as a child that it had percolated into his being and he was able to produce the piece fluidly, without even knowing how it had come to be there. It was as if past, present and future had rolled into one moment of magic—the true, intangible heart of music.

They chatted and shared and played music until the first call to prayer rose out of the inky sky. Putting down his sitar, Joshi babu said, 'Vilayat miyan, do you know this is how I spent so many nights in your house in Calcutta? Your father would put me in charge of your night riyaz. Sometimes, you would fall asleep with your head in my lap, and then your father would call out from the other room, "Has miyan gone to sleep?" I would reply, "No no, he has just gone to the bathroom," and then I would quickly wake you up and get you to start playing again.'

Joshi babu looked across the room at this older miyan, but he was already fast asleep. Vilayat's instrument lay next to him, a hand curled around its stem as if it were a parent.

Joshi babu eventually ended up as a producer at the All India Radio station in Lucknow, and later its deputy chief producer in Delhi, where he worked vigorously to promote and

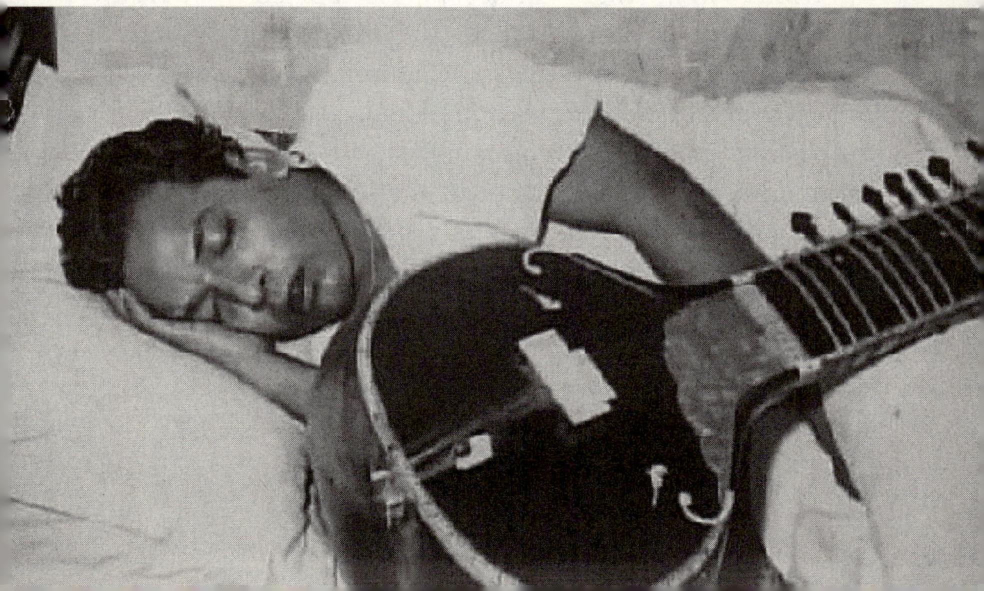

broadcast classical music, indulging Vilayat Khan whenever he could.

Indian families have a comforting way of stepping in during times of trouble. Uncles replace fathers, grandparents take over from parents. After she became a widow, Basheeran Begum's family, also hereditary musicians, welcomed her and her children into their home in Saharanpur for long stretches. The teenaged Vilayat Khan's musical training was taken over by his grandfather Bande Hasan Khan and his beloved mamu, Zinda Hasan Khan.

The grandfather would come to Delhi twice a month to teach him and, once in a while, Vilayat visited him in Saharanpur. His uncle was able to be in Delhi for longer stretches. These two men oxygenated Vilayat's world again. But there was one small difference: they were singers, not sitar players. They taught him music by singing it, and he slowly learned compositions as they were sung, which he translated into his sitar.

Bande Hasan Khan, an accomplished singer as well as wrestler, gave his grandson all the tools he had—which included building his physical stamina. Next to their Saharanpur home, there was an akhada, or wrestling gym. He insisted that Vilayat accompany him there after the morning prayers and go through the full exercise regimen. This, musicians believed, was an equally important part of the musical training, for it made them stronger, especially the hand-wrestle, a pushing exercise called 'zor' to build muscles on their wrist and forearm. Vilayat's grandfather also taught him everything from traditional dhrupad and khayal to the lighter forms of thumri and dadra.

Next to the family home in Saharanpur, separated by a jamun tree, was the house of another musical uncle. One day, as they sat around in the wrestling akhada, this uncle told the young Vilayat the story of how his father Enayat used to visit Saharanpur, and sometimes not leave his room for days. 'No one would see him. He stayed inside with only his drinks and his sitar.' He laughed and said, 'Miyan, you know, one day I was headed outside with my lota and your father was playing Khamaj. "Ab ke aye na balam" … He was playing so beautifully, that I just stood outside for a long time, forgetting what I had set out to do. That was the bewitching magic of Bengal's Jadugar.'

Vilayat Khan's real tutor, however, was his uncle. Zinda Hasan Khan was an unexceptional but passionate singer who was more obsessed with cycling than music. He used to cycle from Delhi to Saharanpur, which would take him more than a day with stops and food breaks. His family remembers how, once, in the middle of the night, they woke up to find him missing. He was nowhere in the house. They went out looking for him and found him in an open field nearby, speeding round and round on his cycle like a man possessed. Zinda mamu had a childlike quality about him. His hair was always dyed orange, the shade depending on when the henna had been last applied.

But Zinda Hasan Khan was not just some eccentric man-child. He was a patient teacher with a musical legacy to back him. He adored his nephew and took it upon himself to teach him vocal music every week in Delhi. That winning combination of love and strictness brought back memories of his father, and Vilayat responded with rigour and devotion. There were times when he would practice all night long without a break, and his mamu would drift in and out of sleep and continue to direct him.

Many great musicians have had teachers who were not

even aware of their role in moulding a genius. Zinda Hasan Khan, a loving, illiterate carrot-top, was one of those mentors, a mere footnote in music history.

Bande Hasan Khan was inside his room one afternoon, listening to his grandson practise raga Kedar in the outer room, but he didn't feel like getting up. So he told his son who was sitting next to him, 'Zinda, can you tell that fool he is not getting the madhyam right. It's the signature note of the raga, tell him not to turn it into keema.'

Zinda ran out of the room, squatted in front of his nephew, and sang the note the correct way.

The old man shouted, once again from inside, 'No, no. You have to pull the madhyam from the dhaivat. Shut your eyes. Listen to yourself. See the notes. You have to learn to gaze beyond the range of your eyes! Smell with your ears, listen with your hands. Then your senses will start making sense!'

Zinda ran back inside to understand exactly what his father meant by that elusive imagery, and then rushed back out to demonstrate it to Vilayat, who spent the next two hours singing and playing just that.

On another occasion, Bande Khan told his grandson, 'You have to be like the alligator. The same sharp teeth with which it carries its young babies are the ones with which it tears apart its prey. Bring that force into your hand—but be equally gentle when the situation demands it.'

Surrounded by the love of uncles and a grandfather, and under the watchful eye of Basheeran Begum, Vilayat felt nurtured again. An unconscious longing to recreate what his father had left, an innate sense of his own talent, and that inexplicable higher force which sparks magic, all conspired to help the young man secure his relationship with music.

As he grew older, Vilayat Khan started accompanying his uncles, who were popular qawwali singers in Saharanpur, to earn a little money on the side. On one such excursion, he was cycling back with his sitar and two earthern pitchers of sugarcane juice, which the concert organisers had given him in addition to the three rupees in fees. It was a particularly hot and humid day. He was lost in the memory of a raga, and didn't see a bump on the road. The next thing he knew, his cycle and he had rolled into a ditch. He had allowed the pitchers to fall on top of him while he protected his instrument.

As he lay there in the mud, scratched and bleeding and covered with sticky sugarcane juice, Vilayat was attacked by a swarm of flies and ants. He looked across the mustard fields, wiped away the marauding insects, and also some tears. As he rolled on to his back with his sitar by his side, the boy remembered his father's words, 'Son, remember that all the ragas of the universe lie inside this wooden instrument. You merely have to release them, one by one.'

He lay there crying until he realised that he would have to twist his cycle back into shape and ride home before it got dark. These were the times when he felt the excruciating absence of a father.

They were not easy times for the family. There was very little money and a cloud of uncertainty hovered over all they did. It is possible that these years of financial insecurity coloured the way way Vilayat Khan lived the rest of his life, even when he was secure and wealthy.

As he grew older, Vilayat started playing small concerts here and there to earn some money, but they were few and far between. He had to stomach periodic bouts of humiliation—like the time he was in Etawah, where his family once had its base. He was invited to play and sing for the local daroga or inspector.

After it was over, Vilayat Khan went up to him and said, 'Can I please have my fees?'

'Fees? How dare you ask me for fees? Do you know who you are talking to? Here are your fees.' And the daroga gave him a slap on his cheek. It was a story he repeated dramatically for many years after.

There was a moment when he was sitting in a tram near Chandni Chowk, in old Delhi, on his way to a sitar-maker's house. At a traffic signal, a sprawling Impala pulled up next to Vilayat. He looked in through the window of the car. Sitting inside was a man with big diamond buttons on his shirt, sparkling in the noon sun. The thought that crossed his mind was, 'Will I ever be able to wear those?'

He was short of cash for days and often did not eat properly. But he was also fiercely proud and never let on that he was hard up. There is another tale that everyone in his family has heard many times over.

Vilayat Khan had been invited to perform at a businessman's home in south Delhi. When he arrived, he walked into a room where a long table was laden with polished silver platters bearing the choicest haleem and biryani and a variety of vegetables. The hosts asked him to join them for dinner before sitting down to play. Even though he was starving, he politely declined. He didn't want to reveal his vulnerability to these people.

'I won't be able to perform on a full stomach, so no thank you,' he said and stepped into the garden where he smoked a beedi to keep his hunger under check.

After the performance, Vilayat took his fees and left, cycling at great speed, to an eating house called Karim's where he often ate. There, he ordered seven different dishes. But his exhaustion was so acute that after gulping down two glasses of water, he lay on the wooden bench and fell asleep.

He woke up a few hours later to the sound of birds welcoming dawn, and the bade miyan who ran the restaurant was stirring something aromatic in a big vat. Vilayat Khan rubbed his eyes and realised how ravenous he was.

'Beta, here is some fresh food for you. Come, eat,' bade miyan said gently.

Vilayat ate the hot food slowly, chewing and relishing every bite. After he was done, bade miyan said, 'Take your baaja and your cycle. I had put them aside for you. Don't worry, you don't have to pay me for the food you didn't eat last night.'

As the young musician was leaving, the old man said, 'Beta, at such a young age, you shouldn't drink that much.' He had assumed that Vilayat fell asleep because he was inebriated.

Sometime later, he was on a train to Calcutta, sitting on the hard wooden seat, with his sitar stowed underneath. His heart ached with that familiar emptiness, letting in waves of fear, anger and sadness. And then, suddenly, without any thought, all the emotions braided themselves into a piece of music.

The man sitting opposite him frowned, for the young Vilayat suddenly smiled like a deranged person, and his fingers started moving, strumming an imaginary instrument. He had entered another world. Vilayat was in the midst of constructing a composition in raga Puriya.

The dark clouds descend, where are you, Enayat?
Why have you abandoned me for another world?
And no longer even ask about me?

Extreme deprivation and formidable talent can be a combustible combination. During these years, Vilayat Khan practised with a tenacity unheard of in a teenager—ten, twelve, fourteen hours at a stretch, under the cold tin roof of Bukhari's garage. When he got tired, he smoked a beedi or drank a glass of milk to replenish his energy, and then went back to playing until his fingers bled. These were the years during which he perfected his technique so that, for the rest of his life, his mind was free and he was able to focus on imagination and ingenuity. His hands would simply follow.

Vilayat Khan fought loneliness by embracing his music. He became the player as well as the listener. One day, he was so intoxicated by his own notes that he finished playing the raga, put his sitar down, got up, straightened his kurta and took a long bow in front of the mirror. He could actually hear the sound of applause around him. The claps grew louder. He smiled and took a slow and deliberate bow again, as if he had just performed in Emperor Akbar's court. Gradually, the concerts of his imagination gave way to real-life concerts and he started getting more invitations to perform.

Around this time, his father's brother, Wahid Khan, who had made a name for himself as a master of surbahar, also started making regular trips from Hyderabad to Delhi to teach Vilayat, and to Calcutta to teach his younger nephew Imrat, spending at least a few days every month with the two of them.

Gradually, the young man acquired exquisite mastery over his instrument; it became an extension of nerve and muscle. By the time he was in his late teens, Vilayat had garnered a reputation for clarity and speed. It is said that Anokhelal Mishra, the tabla player from Banaras, who was known for his own incredible speed when playing the sixteen-beat teental, was astonished at the teenager's pyrotechnics on the instrument. He said, 'Where has this bhoot, this ghost, come from? He is definitely not human!'

When Vilayat Khan left Calcutta as a boy, he had decided

that he would only return as a maestro. On one of his first trips back, he was welcomed warmly by his father's old friend Karamatullah Khan, the tabla player. The two families had been very close, personally and musically.

Karamatullah Khan used to host musical evenings where artistes would gather for music and food. That particular evening, he wanted to present Vilayat to the Calcutta music world. Among those present was Bade Ghulam Ali Khan.

The host turned to the burly Punjabi singer and said, 'With your permission, I'd like to present this young man, Vilayat Hussain Khan, son of Enayat Hussain Khan. Please do pay attention to him.'

Kanhe Maharaj was asked to tune the tabla. Vilayat Khan began playing, and moved quickly into a series of short and stunning taans. Within minutes, Bade Ghulam Ali flew into a rage.

Turning to his host, he said, 'He is playing my music without even asking for my permission. How dare he!'

To everyone's horror, he stopped the young sitar player and started singing a taan in three octaves. To prove a point, he started half a note higher. As he went higher on the scale, his face turned red, his handlebar moustache quivered, and he looked like he would implode. Karamatullah Khan was mortified. He quickly announced that dinner had been served.

Much later that night, a calmer, well-fed Bade Ghulam Ali Khan went up to Vilayat Khan and put an arm around him.

'God bless you, son. If anyone can play my music, it will be you.'

I went to meet the Saharanpur singing side of Vilayat Khan's family. One by one, they had left their home town, where their music would find an audience only in some forgotten mausoleum, and had moved to Mumbai where they were in demand as qawwali singers with the legacy of a gharana, in a film industry perenially hungry for new voices.

They lived in a suburb of Mumbai—an intestine-like coil of confounding lefts and rights off the Western Express Highway. The neighbourhood was faintly moffussil, like one of those tier-three towns. We passed roadside mosques, mirror-and-glass stores and paan shops. Green flags stuck out of walls and nooks every few blocks. As we entered the building gates, the delicious aroma of meat curry enveloped us. We had walked into mini Saharanpur.

This was the home of the Faridis, related to Vilayat Khan from his mother's side of the family, and in several other ways as well, for the families of Muslim musicians are a Byzantine mosaic of criss-crossing relationships. Living here were the descendents of the very qawwal uncles whom the young Vilayat used to accompany as a teenager. Mukarrambhai greeted us warmly and immediately launched into stories about Vilayat Khan.

'I have spent an enormous amount of time with Abba. Every time he came to Bombay, I swooped down on him like a kite,' said Mukarrambhai, fiddling with his plastic rosary beads. 'Our families are very closely linked. Did you know that there was a time when someone had put the evil eye on Abba? He must have been in his forties. It was one of his worst enemies, for he could not even lift his hand, let alone play. Of course, we all knew which sitar player was behind it.'

His brother and sister-in-law touched both their ears as a mark of respect. Others shook their heads, riveted.

'It was Zinda Hasan Khan who saved his life,' continued Mukarrambhai. 'He took his nephew to the mausoleum in Deobandh, along with a maulana, I think it was Bilal miyan.'

'It was Jaleel miyan,' his brother corrected. By now, more family had gathered around and were listening solemnly to this ghostly tale.

'Yes, maybe it was. There, the holy men read some words out for him, gave him a talisman, and said someone has to go to the graveyard in the middle of the night and bury it, but he must not turn back even if he is scared. Zinda bhaiya said he would do anything to save his nephew. "*Meri jaan chali jaye, lekin mera bhanja theek ho jaye.*" (I don't care if I die trying, but my nephew must get better, he announced.)

'That night, Zinda bhaiya heard the terrible wailings of djinns in the dark. He was terrified, but he didn't turn back. He continued on his mission, buried the talisman and returned with a high fever.'

'And was Khansahib cured?' I asked.

'Of course. Mashallah!'

I now met various family members as they flowed out of the rooms. 'This is my son Shahdab who has just sung a qawwali for one of Yashraj-ji's films. And this is Altamash, who also sings for films. Beta, play them your song. And this is Asif,' he said, pointing to a young man who emerged sleepily from inside. 'He just performed qawwali at a farmhouse in Delhi and took an early morning flight back. Everyone is doing well, so I have now stopped singing.'

We heard the music of Yashraj-ji's latest film. It was a remixed qawwali sung by a trained voice, and generations of musicianship clearly came through.

Lunch was served with warmth and a hearty helping of bawdy Urdu poetry. We sat around and listened to more stories about Saharanpur, about Vilayat Khan's days in Dehradun, about the film world and the family's recent Haj visit.

I realised then that Vilayat Khan could easily have been one of them, had he not become Vilayat Khan. How did he manage to shake off his provincial roots—this life of musical mediocrity and religious competitiveness? How did he manage to escape being an invisible tombstone? Where did he develop such sophistication in his music, in the way he dressed, the way he spoke English?

He probably didn't have a choice.

Some people are born with imperatives beyond their control. With them, you can't quite figure out whether the sun is setting or rising. I was now desperate to find out more about this man and how he had fashioned himself into one of India's most charismatic musicians.

CHAPTER THREE

The Frenemy

Since Vilayat Khan had spent most of his youth learning from vocal musicians—his grandfather and uncle—he became a better singer than he was a sitar player. In fact, by the time he reached his late teens, there was a point at which he was so immersed in his singing talents that he even gave several vocal performances. The winning mix of his mellow baritone voice and flawless training struck a chord with listeners.

Basheeran Begum was not pleased with this development and decided to act. She knew the perfect preamble to her intervention. So, she cooked her son's favourite mutton kofta biryani, placed it before him, and very slowly, very deliberately, fanned him while he ate.

'Miyan ...'

'Yes, Amma?'

'I want you to promise me something,' she said.

'Anything you say, Amma.'

'Now listen to me carefully, for what I am about to say is very important.'

'I am listening, Amma.' He laughed, gradually entering a pleasant food daze.

'Promise me you will never ever sing in public again.'

He stopped chewing and looked at his mother, surprised, vaguely hurt.

'Amma?'

'You see, I can easily fold you into my parental gharana; they are well-known singers of Saharanpur and Nahan. Yes, you can easily adopt that lineage.'

She got up, returned with more food from the kitchen, and continued.

'But remember that I am the daughter-in-law of Imdad Khan and the wife of Enayat Khan, and you must always be known as their grandson and son. No one should ever accuse you of abandoning your paternal heritage. Your forefathers have been kings of the sitar for five generations. Therefore, no matter how good you may be as a singer, you must only play the sitar. And your little brother Imrat will play the surbahar.'

Vilayat Khan was distraught. He loved singing. He had taken it for granted that singing would be a part of his life. When he next met his Zinda mamu, Vilayat was visibly depressed. He told his mamu about the conversation with Amma. Zinda Hasan Khan was about to go on one of his long cycle rides. He told his nephew to sit and practise till he returned.

About an hour later, Zinda mamu returned to see Vilayat sitting on the steps looking forlorn. He went up to his nephew and put a hand on his shoulder.

'Look, Miyan, I know my sister very well. She is not going to relent. So, instead of singing, just make your sitar sing. It's really quite simple.'

Vilayat stared at his mamu in disbelief. Something extraordinary had just taken place, though the world would not receive it till much later.

The two then went inside. Zinda mamu dabbed his face with the end of his scarf and sat down with his tanpura. Vilayat

Khan sat quietly in front of him, feeling humble and grateful and suddenly relieved.

'Miyan, have you heard the name Rahimsen?' asked Zinda mamu. 'He was one of the great sitar players. He came from a family of Dhrupad singers, but after his father died, he felt that no one was good enough to teach him. So he decided to turn to his father-in-law, Dhula Khan, a sitar player, who said to him, "Yes, the sitar isn't worth two cents compared to Dhrupad. Dhrupad is a jewel and sitar is just a pebble, but I will change this pebble to equal a jewel." And you know, Rahimsen applied thought and effort, and he filled the sitar with veena, dhrupad and khayal styles, and soon great musicians bowed their heads before his sitar … You have great talent, Miyan, you can do anything you want.'

With tears in his eyes, Vilayat kissed his mamu on both cheeks and then ran out to kiss the sky.

Over the next few years, he started doing something extraordinary, working both unconsciously and consciously. He meticulously created and nurtured the gayaki ang, or the vocal style, in instrumental music. His sitar began to emulate that most vital and primal mode of human expression—the voice.

By improving his left-hand technique, Vilayat Khan was able to bend and sustain notes for long stretches, thus modulating and touching those unseen half and quarter notes that only the voice can cajole out. He added a narrative quality to the music, building the slow alaap with emotion, and great variations in volume, timbre and pace, all derived from the world of vocal music. He used pauses and silent spaces very subtly, almost simulating the process of a singer's breathing. He once said, 'When I sit down on stage to play, everything comes to me in the form of a vocal performance. I never planned this. It just happens. My sitar then sings.'

Vilayat Khan did not merely play his sitar. He sang through it. It was this distinctive quality that made him, arguably, a finer player than his lifelong adversary—Ravi Shankar.

Perhaps every great artiste or sportsman needs a rival—someone to shadow box with, to bring out the best in them, to pull them out of complacency, to create a sense of self against a second-best. Vilayat Khan first met the person who would be his bête noire in Delhi, sometime in the 1940s, when he was

a teenager working at All India Radio. The encounter took place in the home of the Shriram–Shankarlal family.

They lived on Curzon Road, in two adjoining palatial houses separated by a skating rink, a swimming pool and a goat pen. Apart from building industrial empires, the Shriram–Shankarlals were generous supporters of the performing arts, inspired by an exciting new nationalist fervour. Having musicians teach them and stay in their home was as much a status symbol as owning an imported car.

The sitar first found its way into the Curzon Road home when some members of the family started learning from Baba Allauddin Khan. A corner room in the big house came to be known as 'Baba ka kamra', a space where he stayed, practised and taught. But since Baba couldn't be in Delhi for long stretches, as his proxy he brought in the bright young student who would eventually become his son-in-law.

His name was Ravi Shankar.

One afternoon, Baba, his daughter Annapurna Devi, Ravi Shankar and some of the Shrirams were sitting around the big horseshoe-shaped rosewood dining table in the house when Lala Shriram's young son Bharat Ram switched on the wireless radio. It crackled into the room and, within seconds, all conversation came to a halt because of the scintillating strumming that emerged from the box. It was raga Pilu. The final bits were breathtaking.

'Subhanallah!' Baba said softly into the silence that followed the performance. 'Who is this?'

'Let's find out. We can send for the artiste. The station is only five minutes away,' said Bharat Ram.

The family Dodge was sent to Akashvani Bhavan. It returned with a handsome young man, wearing a black kurta, loose pajamas and rimless spectacles. He said his salaams and didn't smile much.

'You are Enayat's elder son?'

'Yes, Baba.'

'Your hand is supremely pakka, my boy. Well played.'

'Thank you.'

'I know your father is no more, God bless his soul, but if you ever want to continue your training, please come to me. It will be my privilege to teach the great Enayatbhai's son. We have spent so many wonderful times together.'

'Yes, Baba, certainly. Thank you.'

Vilayat Khan never returned to learn from him. But he did go across to the house a couple of times to play ping-pong with Bharat Ram's eldest son Vinay, who had by then become Ravi Shankar's devoted student.

On a brilliant afternoon sometime in early 1947, Ravi Shankar, Ali Akbar Khan and the Shrirams were sitting around the same rosewood table, chatting about the imminence of Indian independence. Four bearers stood behind them, still as statues. Among those present was Lala Shriram's daughter-in-law, Sumitra Charat Ram, who would soon become patron queen of the performing arts.

'Lalaji, India is getting its independence, let us mark this great day with a grand musical celebration,' said Ravi Shankar.

Lala Shankarlal, the music lover in the family, nodded enthusiastically.

'It's a great idea, Robu-da,' said Sumitra Charat Ram. 'You will, of course, perform. And who else shall we get?' She turned around and addressed one of the bearers. 'Shamsher Singh, can you please bring a pen?'

They drew up a list, getting more and more excited with

each name they wrote down: every one of them the biggest musicians of the time. Bade Ghulam Ali Khan, Hafiz Ali Khan, Amir Khan, Mushtaq Husain Khan.

The concert was held on the eve of Independence in the grand hall of their home. The entire house was lit up as if it were a wedding. From five in the evening, horse carriages and foreign cars filed into the massive portico, ferrying Delhi's elite—musicians, businessmen, politicians. One guest whispered to his wife that this was the house where Jawaharlal Nehru once hid in the basement to escape the British.

They called the event 'Jhankar'. It was such an enormous success that the family started hosting the festival on a regular basis at different historic venues across Delhi, including the Red Fort and the Constitution Club, where it became more or less permanently fixed. Within a few years, the Shrirams had formed the Bharatiya Kala Kendra, a performing arts academy, and the Jhankar Festival became a permanent annual feature. This was where India's greatest artistes performed to an audience of passionate connoisseurs.

It was at a Jhankar concert in 1952 that Vilayat Khan stormed in to play with Ravi Shankar, pushing their relationship to a point from which there was no going back. Vilayat Khan was declared the de facto victor in the battle of the sitars.

As for the relationship between Ravi Shankar and Vilayat Khan and the Shriram–Shankarlal family, that too slowly morphed into a triangle of ambivalent love. The Shrirams were devoted to Ravi Shankar. They were equally in awe of the genius of Vilayat Khan—but not enough, according to the maestro himself.

Ravi Shankar and Vilayat Khan had two things in common—mastery over their instrument and unabashed self-absorption. But they came from very different worlds, which perhaps shaped the way they approached their music.

The identity that Ravi Shankar fashioned for himself was nothing like that of a traditional Indian musician. Even as a very young man, he viewed himself as an international star rather than an Indian pandit of music.

Rabindra Shankar Chowdhury's father, Shyam Shankar, was an educated and accomplished man of letters—a scholar of Sanksrit, a barrister-at-law at the Middle Temple in London, and later a lecturer at Columbia University in New York. Shyam Shankar left his wife and very young children in Banaras, and then went on to have a series of affairs with English women.

Ravi Shankar's childhood was spent in Banaras, but when he was in his early teens, his elder brother Uday Shankar whisked Ravi off to Paris to work in his ballet company. Ravi's most formative years unfolded in the bohemian clubs of Europe in a heady world inhabited by dancers and musicians. He spent two years at a French school and went on many trips across the continent. Long before he returned to India to connect with the spartan world of classical Indian music, he had romped around the cobbled streets of Paris.

In 1934, when Ravi Shankar was fourteen—and in Calcutta, getting increasingly drawn to Indian music—two events changed the course of his musical life. He had lost the opportunity to learn with Enayat Khan, but was still determined to find a teacher of classical music, which he did a few months later at the All-Bengal Music Conference in Calcutta. He heard the grand master, an ambidexterous musician who could play a range of instruments and was known for introducing an eclecticism hitherto unknown in the classical music world. He was dressed in a simple dhoti and tunic, and his goatee was dyed jet black. This was Baba Allauddin Khan.

Baba was then a court musician at Maihar, a small kingdom south of Banaras, where the whimsical raja had instructed him to conjure up a small orchestra of instrumental music. He managed to get a bunch of orphan boys into musical shape—not without a few beatings—and taught them both Indian and Western instruments, including a half-banjo half-sitar mutant that he had invented. At the All-Bengal Music Conference, the Maihar orchestra played both classical and light pieces and was applauded for its virtuosity. The next day Ustad Allauddin Khan himself performed on the sarod, accompanied by his twelve-year-old son Ali Akbar Khan, who would later become a musical brother to both Ravi Shankar and Vilayat Khan.

Around this time, Uday Shankar convinced Baba to join his ballet troupe for some performances in Europe. They met up in Bombay and rehearsed for a few weeks before taking off. Ravi Shankar returned from the tour to become a full-time student of Baba's.

At a very young age, Ravi had a sense of being a global citizen, rather than a Bengali or even an Indian. When he started performing on All India Radio, he changed his name to Ravi from Rabindra. He wrote in his autobiography, *Raga Mala*: 'Ravi Shankar sounded just right, and that was how I told the announcers to introduce me on the radio. All India Radio was heard throughout India, so people came to know me by my new name. Anyone who was not aware that I was a Bengali always thought I was from United Provinces (now Uttar Pradesh) or Rajasthan or Gujarat. That was what I wanted. I am proud to be a Bengali, but it made me more international, in the Indian sense.'

In 1948, when Ravi Shankar was not yet thirty, he became music director of All India Radio with the additional role of composer–conductor of its new instrumental ensemble. Three years later, he launched the national orchestra, Vadya Vrinda, including in it an extraordinary medley of instruments—sitar, sarod, veena, flute, sarangi, shahnai, and violin, cello, double bass and clarinet. He introduced new ideas of harmony to India's auditory palette.

Gradually, thanks to his growing popularity, the sitar itself became universal, finding its way into popular films, restaurants, elevators, and becoming a part of the country's musical consciousness.

The elegant long-necked sitar was not always so popular. Like most things in India, this instrument has various origin stories. One school of thought attributes its invention to Amir Khusrau, the mystic musician who came to India in the thirteenth century, bringing with him elements from Persia. Another suggests that it is a descendent of the rudra veena or the been, an old Indian instrument often found in images of gods, for it has similar physical attributes—long-stemmed, wooden, with two gourds on either side.

The contemporary sitar has a wooden stem and the gourd is made of dried pumpkin. It is played by plucking with a plectrum or mizrab. There are seven strings and numerous additional sympathetic or tarab strings under the main strings, pulled over a small flat bridge called jawari. These are tuned to the particular raga being played to enrich the sound. There are usually twenty frets along the stem.

Around the mid-nineteenth century, an instrument that loosely fell between the veena and the sitar also came into being—the surbahar, a bass sitar, with a heavier, more sombre sound. The surbahar is to the sitar what the cello might be to the violin. Vilayat Khan used to claim that his great-grandfather Sahebdad Khan contributed to the invention of this instrument. The veracity of all this is questionable, but like most of India's oral history, no one is an owner; the arts belong to the practitioner—and the universe.

Most sitar players were also trained to play the surbahar. Alauddin Khan chose to teach the surbahar to his daughter Annapurna Devi. While they were married, she and Ravi Shankar performed many duets of sitar and surbahar.

The wise Basheeran Begum had decided very early on that her elder son Vilayat would play the sitar and her younger, Imrat, would play the surbahar, demarcating territories, much as a patriarch might carve out two separate land holdings for his sons. By doing this, she also ensured that the legacy of both instruments stayed alive. Her foresight was remarkable. When she was a young and sudden widow, left impoverished and bereft, someone had tried to buy her husband's surbahar but she refused to sell it. This was going to be her younger son's legacy.

Over the years, the surbahar receded from the public imagination. It was the sitar that eventually caught on, because of its versatility and easy melodic qualities. By the mid-twentieth century, the two major streams of sitar were the Maihar gharana, represented by Ravi Shankar, and the Etawah gharana, named after the original home of Vilayat Khan's ancestors. Other stylistic schools in sitar include the Indore gharana, the contemporary master of which was Abdul Halim Jaffer Khan. There was also Nikhil Banerjee, a master sitar player whose music has been described as a happy medium between the Vilayat Khan and the Ravi Shankar schools.

Yet, for the world at large, the sitar became synonymous

with two words: Raaaavi Shankerr, which is how the Western world said his name.

Because they were contemporaries, Ravi Shankar—or, more specifically, his maddening fame—remained an undercurrent in Vilayat's life. Even though music lovers discreetly spoke of Vilayat Khan's music with more reverence, the masses were not as discerning. This would often drive Khansahib crazy. Over the years, his bitter references to Ravi Shankar became legendary and people just learned to roll their eyes or take sides.

And yet, both had tremendous respect for each other.

While researching this book, I kept trying to find that sensational angle which would transform a boring biography into a page-turner, and the one that seemed most obvious was the rivalry between the two sitar players, which I could fashion into an epic story, as Milos Forman did with Antonio Salieri and Amadeus Mozart in the film *Amadeus*.

But then I realised that every musician makes choices, and Vilayat Khan had very deliberately chosen a certain path, one that looked within for depth rather than beyond, one that was solitary rather than collaborative. It would not lead to sharing record sleeves with famous pop stars, and it would not make him famous among the musically naive. But it is what he chose. He served as a reminder that there are spaces more intoxicating than fame. As Hans Utter wrote, compared to Ravi Shankar, Vilayat Khan made his life and art 'a narrative of resistance'.

CHAPTER FOUR

A Rock Star Is Born

It was in Bombay, in 1944, that Vilayat Khan went from being a seventeen-year-old shy man-boy to becoming a dapper maestro.

The Vikramaditya Music Conference—a grand seven-day-long celebration of live music with artistes from all over the country—was propitious for Vilayat's career. The conference featured the young and upcoming, the old and revered. They all came with colourful entourages of students, acolytes, accompanists, sons and lovers. Season tickets were sold in advance and cost between thirty and 200 rupees.

It was the second-last day of the music conference. The early morning sun filtered into the arched stained-glass windows of the University Convocation Hall, a stunning gothic structure built by the British in the Fort area of Bombay, where the performances were to take place. Inside, a man was arranging the chairs in neat rows. A young tabla player called Nikhil Ghosh was wandering around the grounds, excited to be a part of this historic event. The previous day, he had accompanied his brother Pannalal Ghosh, a master on the flute. Nikhil-da was still high from listening to legends like Omkarnath Thakur, Rasoolanbai, Faiyaz Khan ... The next morning would bring the programme to a close with the grand old man of vocal music, Alladiya Khan. He pictured the maestro's giant white whiskers and smiled.

As he stood in one corner of the building, looking out at the palms on the street, Nikhil-da heard an electrifying strumming. He had not heard this sound before. It was as if sitar, sarangi and human voice had been rolled into one—a plucking instrument actually sustaining the space between the notes that only the bow or voice could achieve.

He stopped to listen, hand instinctively stroking his beard. Like a man enchanted, he started walking towards the music and found his way to a room behind the concert hall.

Sitting with a sitar, facing the wall, was a young man. He could only see the musician in profile and did not recognise him. Nikhil-da stood there listening, amazed at this man's tenacity, his hand movements, the way he repeated a single sapat phrase again and again and again with ferocious determination. He had never encountered such effortless mastery of the instrument. The musician finally stopped and turned around. Behind his glasses, the young man's eyes were on fire.

'Who are you, khoka?'

'I am Vilayat Hussain Khan from Calcutta.'

Nikhil-da congratulated him on his playing and they became instant friends, breaking into Bengali. They chatted about music and about musicians they had heard and liked, or really liked, at the conference. They talked about the new young singer from Patiala, Ghulam Ali Khan, and about the Saraswati veena played by a court musician from Mysore, which had been the opening act.

A few minutes later, the tabla master Ahmed Jan Thirakwa walked into the room and sternly asked the young sitar player to get ready for his performance. It was clear from the tabla legend's manner that he had known the sitarist all his life. He would be accompanying Vilayat, just as he had accompanied his father and grandfather, Thirakwa told Nikhil-da.

'I played tabla with this lad the first time he sat on a stage in Calcutta, when he was barely eight or nine years old,' he said, patting the younger man's back affectionately when Vilayat bent to touch his feet. 'I promised his father I would take care of him and here I am.'

Later that morning, Vilayat Khan was a sensation on stage. Even the most discerning connoisseurs had never heard the sitar played this way. The sound was electric, his speed spectacular. But it was not just that. There was something unique about the way in which he ornamented his music. It was almost as if the instrument was human. His sitar was singing.

Vilayat concluded his concert to a standing ovation, and a few people from the audience spontaneously ran up on stage and lifted him up to loud cheers. Overnight, the Vikramaditya Conference changed everything. It was a landmark professional triumph.

A few weeks after this concert, Vilayat was so charged by his heady success that he is rumoured to have picked up his sitar and held it horizontally like a machine gun. '*Dhaar dhaar dhaar dishoom. Mera muqabala kaun karega?* Who wants to take me on now?' he cried, pointing it this way and that.

Sometime later, Films Division, a government-owned film production house, made a documentary which featured Ahmed Jan Thirakwa, Govindrao Bhuranpurkar, both percussionists, Pannalal Ghosh and the young Vilayat Khan. Curiously, no vocalists were included.

The Vikramaditya Conference marked another important musical milestone. The sitar was suddenly taken seriously as a performance instrument, on par with vocal music. Until this point, there had been a subtle snobbery towards instrumental music and musicians. They were considered 'mirasis', a derogatory term for wandering musicians; they were also paid less by patrons. The sitar had always been a lower player in the pecking order and sitar players had to strive to prove themselves to be as accomplished as the masters of voice. Even radio broadcasts gave instrumentalists far less transmission time compared to vocal music or Western classical music.

Among instruments too, some were considered more respectable than others, based on how difficult they were to play. This is possibly why Vilayat Khan's grandfather Imdad Khan, who played the sarangi as well as the jaltarang, preferred to be known for the sitar and surbahar.

All this was about to change.

By the early twentieth century, Bombay, like Calcutta, had become a significant centre for music. Princely patronage across India had diminished and merchant princes were the new maharajas—wealthy and culturally aspirational. Unlike Calcutta, where Bengalis and Marwaris monopolised the new aristocracy, Bombay had a cosmopolitan elite that consisted of Parsis, Maharashtrians, Gujaratis, Kutchi Bhatias, and anyone who wanted to participate in building the commercial centre of a bright new India.

Bombay's music scene had been going through a long lull, but three visionaries—a Parsi and two Maharashtrian Hindus—helped revive it. In 1870, a journalist, scholar and social reformer called Kaikhushro Kabraji started a performing arts club, the Parsi Gayan Uttejak Mandali in the Foras Road neighbourhood. This was then the city's red light district and also home to some of the greatest musicians, given the blurry lines between those two worlds. The Mandali initially catered to the Parsi community, but soon opened its doors to non-Parsis. It attracted many professional musicians, including Dada Imdad Khan, as teachers.

Among the students who joined the Parsi Gayan Uttejak Mandali was Vishnu Narayan Bhatkhande, a young lawyer who was passionate about music. At the Mandali, he learnt hundreds of traditional compositions and also was exposed to different musical styles. Bhatkhande then did something extraordinary: he painstakingly gathered compositions from musicians all over India and devised a notation system, applying Western scientific systems of documenting knowledge to what had been an oral tradition.

Experiments in notation of Indian music had been carried out earlier in Calcutta and Baroda, but Bhatkhande's contribution was far-reaching. Many musicians may not have been able to identify the precise notes they were singing. Now, for the first time, the grammar of their music was being analysed and written.

Bhatkhande democratised music. Suddenly, the world at large had access to a master's secrets. He created a curriculum for its mass education, which was eventually incorporated in the municipal schools of Bombay. Underlying this was, perhaps, also a Brahminical intervention to sanitise an art form that many felt had been cheapened because of the tawaif or courtesan tradition. Children from middle-class homes could now start learning music as it was considered a part of 'culture', not merely 'entertainment'. By the time he died, on Ganesh Chaturthi day in 1936, Bhatkhande had created not only a new breed of musicians but also brand-new audiences.

Gradually, north Indian classical music became widely accessible in Bombay. It also became a medium for Indians to start feeling good about their own art forms, instead of adopting and keeping up with English customs. Music became the space for a new assertion through culture.

Around the same time, another Vishnu was committed to the same idea—of bringing respectability to Indian music, and also of creating a wide audience. Vishnu Digambar Paluskar, a singer from Sangli, a princely state in Maharashtra, established the Gandharva School of Music, initially in Lahore and eventually in Bombay, in 1908. He set up several branches across the city, under Kennedy Bridge and in Kalbadevi in Bombay, and in the neighbouring cities of Pune and Nagpur. The Gandharva Vidyalaya soon became a well-regarded chain of music schools.

This highly motivated, almost blind man also launched a series of annual music conferences in Bombay, showcasing performers, featuring exhibitions on instruments, and hosting discussions and seminars. The conferences were often inagurated by an eminent city personality to create an aspirational pull, and members of the public attended in large numbers. Artistes were paid honorariums to perform, and didn't have to rely on the generosity or whim of some patron. Paluskar himself used to charge the substantial sum of 500 rupees for a single appearance. Tickets at the time cost anywhere between one and five rupees. These concerts are considered the precursors of present-day public concerts.

Musicians have always tweaked and altered their compositions to cater to new patrons: while earlier compositions were in praise of the maharajas, now the songs changed to acknowledge the new benefactors. In his book, *Hindustani Music in Colonial Bombay*, the musician and scholar Aneesh Pradhan writes that, in 1907, the feisty Gauhar Jaan sang in Bombay's Town Hall a song praising the philanthropy of Bombay's rich businessmen, even naming some of them in the lyrics.

Rahe abad ya rab Bambai aur Bambai vale
Kahan main ek musafir aur kahan yeh qasar sultanee
(I, an insignificant visitor to this magnificent edifice
Pray that Bombay and its citizens may forever prosper)

By and by, other music circles started in the city—such as the Bombay Music Circle and the Musical Arts Society, which held the Vikramaditya Conference.

Whereas his father found refuge in the princely court of Gowripur, it is hardly surprising that an ambitious young man like Vilayat Khan would move to Bombay and ensconce himself in this exciting world filled with impoverished but amazing musicians and a hungry new elite, both feeding off each other. There was also the burgeoning film industry, which had billowed across the city and absorbed many classical musicians into its fold. Many, many artistes migrated to the city by the sea, like flamingos in search of food.

❧

When he first came to Bombay, Vilayat Khan stayed with his older sister Naseeran, who was married to Mohammed Khan, a gentle man and gifted sitar player who had become popular in Mumbai circles as an ace teacher. His students included the actor Raj Kapoor and a well-regarded dentist, Dr Ratnakar Shamsie. They lived in a flat near the Islam Gymkhana at Chowpatty with their little boy Rais Khan and three daughters.

After the success of the Vikramaditya Conference, Vilayat Khan started getting invited to perform at the big festivals as well as to private concerts in and around Bombay. Armed with his new confidence and earning power, he moved his mother and younger siblings to Bombay sometime in the late 1940s, just before Independence.

They first moved to a tiny place in Kalyan, a suburb of Bombay, where their uncle Wahid Khan lived, because that was all they could afford. This was when Wahid Khan started teaching Imrat the surbahar in a more systematic manner. They then briefly lived in a tiny flat near the old Strand Cinema in Colaba. Later, they moved to Bhujwari Mohalla on Zakaria Street off Mohammed Ali Road, close to Crawford Market, into another tiny flat which was up four flights of stairs so dark that it was difficult to climb up without running into some little creature.

These were the years when Vilayat Khan became mentor and teacher to his young brother Imrat, a sweet mild-mannered boy eight years younger than him. Imrat was barely ten or twelve when they moved to Zakaria Street. He doted on his elder brother and was his little foot soldier, ensuring Vilayat's clothes were always washed and ironed and his shoes polished to a shine. He would run up and down the stairs all day long to bring his 'bade bhaiya' beedis and anything else he needed from the market.

When Vilayat Khan returned home late after a night of music or revelry, he would mumble, 'Imrat ...' The boy would jump up and, in his drowsy state, massage and pound his brother's back until they both fell into deep sleep. Sometimes, while his young brother was sitting on his back, Vilayat Khan would chat with him, grunting while his brother pushed and pummelled, telling him about the ragas he had played that evening and how the nishad in his Yaman Kalyan had brought tears to people's eyes.

When he was not doing things for his brother, Imrat would follow his mother around, helping her with chores. Circumstances had extinguished the possibility that he might still go to school, but Basheeran Begum ensured that Imrat's education in music lived up to the family legacy; there was no compromise in that department.

Although Vilayat Khan was getting busy with his own emerging career, she insisted that he spend time at night teaching Imrat. They played for hours together, practising through the night, repeating phrases, learning ragas. Vilayat was protective of his young brother but also impatient with him, and refused to repeat anything more than once. Imrat blindly followed his brother's instructions, never getting upset when his brother scolded him.

'You will never be able to play, you gadha, you donkey; we will have to open a paan shop for you, Imrat miyan,' was Vilayat's regular refrain.

Every once in a while, their mother would remind her elder son to be gentler on the boy. And she would tell Imrat,

'He is not your elder brother, he is both your father and your teacher now.'

Just as Basheeran Begum had ensured that her elder son got the best training possible, she now did the same for her younger son. Vilayat would be away for long stretches of time, either performing or partying, not always with musicians. Her back-up plan involved strategically enticing a host of teachers, each of whom came with his own eccentricities, which she managed with the ease of a tiger mom.

While Imrat's training came largely from his father's brother, Wahid Khan, she also started inviting her husband's old friend Khadim Hussain Khan, a well-known singer of the Rampur gharana, to the flat. He was an unusually emotional man and would often burst into tears when reminiscing about his late friend Enayat. She would then shut him up: 'If you really love him, teach his son. No point in all this drama!'

She would cook Khadim Khan's favourite food to keep him coming. After he ate, he would call Imrat to sit in front of him, bring out the round dagga and play it with his left hand, with a beedi stuck permanently between his fingers.

But this was not enough. The wily Basheeran then came up with another idea. She knew that her husband's nephew, Hafiz Khan Mastana, the son of Wahid Khan, had trained substantially under her husband when he was young and lived with them in the Park Circus house. But Hafiz Khan, or Babbu as he was known in the family, had long since left classical music behind and plunged into the heady world of Hindi films where, as Khan Mastana, he had a short but successful stint as a composer until alcohol and marijuana took over and he lost almost everything.

Basheeran Begum shamelessly exploited his condition and started encouraging him to come and teach her son, in return giving him the money he needed to feed his addictions. Although Khan Mastana had stopped playing the sitar, his early training in music was thorough. He taught his young cousin Imrat by singing, directing him while the boy played.

The times were not easy, but thanks to his mother's persistence, Imrat slowly learned the music that eventually made him a formidable surbahar player. Gradually, he could both play solo as well as shadow and accompany his brilliant elder brother, which is what he did for many years until ... But that's a story for later.

Sometime in the late 1940s or early 1950s, the family settled into Zakaria Street and Bombay became home. The main room was divided by a sari that hung from a string in the middle. On one side of the room was a sofa opposite two folding chairs, so close that if you sat across from each other, your feet almost touched; on the other side of the partition, Amma cooked, sprinkling her food with a generous dose of venom against whoever happened to fall foul of her that day.

One particular afternoon, she was lashing out at Amir Khan, a singer known for his deep baritone and contemplative style, who also happened to be her son-in-law. Amir Khan was originally from Indore, where his father served as the court's sarangi player, but had moved to Calcutta and then Bombay. He married Vilayat Khan's sister Zeenat, who was more than a decade younger than him. They had a baby daughter, Fehmida. But Amir Khan was a loner and a concert artiste. He was never home. Their marriage lasted barely two years, and by the time she was eighteen, Zeenat was back home with her mother.

'I forbid any of you to keep ties with him after the break-up,' said Basheeran to an assortment of family. 'Why I married my girl to this foolish sarangi-playing beggar, I don't know. She must leave him as soon as possible. It's all the fault of Abbajan, who couldn't see beyond Shahmir,' she said.

She was referring to Amir Khan's father, Shahmir Khan, who was her father Bande Hasan Khan's dearest friend. 'Yes, yes, we all know he's a great singer, but such a nikamma, he doesn't even have money to replace a dead light bulb or buy his wife soap. He roams around in a trance of his own, as if he is the great Abdul Karim Khansahib himself.'

She went on and on, her contempt fuelled by her audience's silent disapproval of it. Vilayat Khan was slowly chewing his food, not enjoying the taste, not saying a word in response, his ears burning from his mother's atonal outburst, his heart sinking. Amir Khan had been his closest friend—in Delhi, when they were both young impoverished students together, and in Saharanpur, where they both learned from Bande Hasan Khan, getting their ears tweaked by the great masters. Now they were both in Bombay, where Amir Khan had also moved after marrying Vilayat's beloved Zeenat apa. He adored the man who was almost a foot taller than him—in height, in music.

Vilayat Khan had heard so many stories about how Bande Hasan Khan and Shahmir Khan would roam around 'Bombay Bazar' in Indore, virile turbans standing tall on their heads, sexy surma lining their eyes, clutching red roses, in search of companions for the evening. This was where the city's talented dancing and singing girls lived and entertained. Every evening, when the sun went down, the area became redolent with incense and music. Some of the best sarangi players and tabaliyas lived and worked here. Walking through the narrow lanes, the two men would pull each other's leg. 'Oye

Shahmire, the gorgeous Gokibai is leaning out of her window and looking me up this fine evening.' To which Shahmir Khan would reply, 'Don't be fooled, bhaijan! She is checking me out, not you!'

Besides inheriting a close friendship, Vilayat and Amir also had a strong musical link. When Shahmir Khan had requested of Bande Hasan Khan that he teach Amir vocal music, Vilayat's grandfather had instantly tied the thread that made the boy his student. The two boys learned together, and the commingling of styles became a common thread in their music.

Amir Khan used to confide in his friend how he slowly and painfully made the transition from sarangi player to singer, unlearning and learning, bearing taunts from others, and most of all from his own inner critic. There were times when one had no money in his pocket, and the other bought tea and biscuits.

Most of all, Vilayat Khan craved time with Amir Khan because there was a depth of serenity in Amir's music, which was the very element missing in his own. The idea of not seeing him was painful, for Amir Khan, more than fifteen years older than him, gave Vilayat the tranquillity that had eluded him because of age and circumstance. Vilayat's insecurities and restless spirit had turned him into a showman who played with startling vigour and speed, but lacked the quiet controlled elegance that existed in his friend's music. Their tabla player friend Mohammed Ahmed used to joke that Amir Khan used to sing at such a slow tempo that, between two beats of his alaap, one could finish a cup of tea. Vilayat Khan knew he had to be around Amir Khan to imbibe that serenity. He could manage without his girlfriends, his drink even, but he couldn't bear the thought of not having this friend in his life. Amir Khan breathed music. It was the only language he spoke, even when he was not singing. Merely talking to him was like taleem, like being in a music class.

Yet, what could Vilayat do? His mother dictated most things in his life and he could not bear to displease her.

Tentatively, he said, 'Amma, did you know that All India Radio delayed its news bulletin because bhaisahib took a little extra time to wind up his Bageshree the other night.'

'I don't care, Miyan. Please do not have anything to do with him.'

'Yes, Amma,' he said quietly, and left the house. He walked some way along the stretch that led towards Marine Drive and sat on the promenade by the sea, one of the few places that gave him peace. He watched the waves move back and forth, reminded of the way Amir Khan delivered his khayal where, before one note had receded, the other came on.

Besides music, they shared a love for Urdu poetry and spent many hours listening to verses in various mehfils. One October evening, they were both standing outside the Laxmi Baug concert hall in Bombay. Amir Khan spoke in the slow cadence of an alaap.

'Bhai, you know, while coming here, I walked past a saptaparni tree. At least, I think that is what it was. The heady fragrance intoxicated me for those few seconds, but I continued on my way, realising its beauty only in the aftertaste. And I remembered my favourite poem. You know, the one by Malihabadi…

Gunche teri zindagi pe dil hilta hai
sirf ek tabassum ke liye khilta hai.
Gunche ne kaha ki, is chaman mein baba
ye ek tabassum bhi kise milta hai

'If you can blossom and give your listener even one chance to smile, it is well worth it, dear brother. How many have even that in their destiny … Remember that music must never be separated from nature and from the divine. It cannot merely be a medium to please the masses. Never sing or play for your audience. Treat this with sanctity ... let it be like the beautiful flower that blossoms, making people's heads turn. Or like the wispy smoke of incense which floats above both the musician and the listener and leaves an aroma long after.'

The two men had long periods of separation, but they would always return to each other. By and by, as her boys grew older and her girls were suitably betrothed, Basheeran Begum started spending more time in Calcutta, at the Park Circus house, and Vilayat Khan continued to meet Amir Khan whenever he could.

By the mid-1940s, Vilayat Khan settled down in Bombay and started teaching regularly. His students were often rich young businessmen who wanted a taste of life's finer offerings. Classical musicians earned their living teaching these aspirants, many of whom were from Gujarat and Kutch. The fees from concerts were not enough to pay for their families and their indulgences. While women singers like Kesarbai and Mogubai could rely on patrons to support them, male musicians like Vilayat Khan, Pulin Dev Burman, Khadim Hussain Khan, Niyaz Ahmed, Faiyaz Ahmed Khan and Mohammed Khan attached themselves to wealthy business families.

In 1944, when they were both about eighteen, Vilayat Khan met Arvind Parikh, a young man from one such Gujarati business family. Arvind had been learning sitar from one Makarand Badshah in Ahmedabad and was visiting Bombay for a radio audition. When his uncle asked if he wanted to meet the young sitar star Vilayat Khan, Arvind jumped at the offer. He was instructed to show up at his uncle's home on Marine Drive at 11.30 the next morning. Arvind arrived half an hour early. At 11.30 a.m. sharp, the doorbell rang and, in place of the bearded ustad he had imagined, stood a handsome young man wearing a suit and tinted glasses, with an unlit cigarette in his mouth. Was he a musician or a movie star, thought Arvind.

'So you play the sitar? Play something for me?' said Vilayat Khan, his eyes twinkling. 'Play what you were planning to present at your radio audition.'

Arvind sat down and confidently started raga Yaman on an instrument that was blithely out of tune. A few minutes into the music, Vilayat Khan stopped him and started singing a Yaman composition. 'Come, try playing this.'

Arvind listened carefully and played it back. Vilayat Khan realised that this young man and his tuneless instrument were not going to pass the audition. He picked up the telephone and dialled the number of the music coordinator at the radio station. 'Dinkarji, my friend Arvind Parikh is coming for an audition this evening, please look after him.'

Arvind returned to Ahmedabad and received a letter stating that 'the performance did not meet the requirements of the microphone'. Vilayat's kind words were not enough to make up for the shortfall in virtuosity.

But Arvind was determined. He met Vilayat Khan again the next year, soon after the heady Vikramaditya Conference debut, and begged the young Khansahib to take him on as a student. Arvind got admission to Elphinstone College and moved to Bombay. Every afternoon, after college, he would drive across to pick up his teacher from Chowpatty, where he was staying with his sister. On most days, Vilayat's insolent nephew Rais Khan would curtly inform him that Mamu was not home. Arvind enrolled as a member of the Hindu Gymkhana next door, and started playing billiards to while away time while waiting for his teacher to get home. In between his games, he would keep returning to Mohammed Khan's house to see if the young ustad had returned, until he finally found him and drove him to a relative's flat in Breach Candy where they had their lessons.

Those few months of waiting turned Arvind into an ace billiards player if not yet a sitar player. But his patience proved to be worth it because, gradually, the lessons became longer and more regular, sometimes continuing late into the night. Vilayat Khan was testing his student to see whether this was just a rich kid with a passing fancy for music he could show off to his friends, or one who had the commitment and tenacity it takes to fall into this bottomless–topless world. It took about six months of billiards for Vilayat Khan to sense that the interest was genuine, and worth his time as well as Arvind's.

When he taught, Vilayat Khan sat opposite Arvind and sang. That was how he had been taught, so that was what emerged naturally, for there are no rules in this world, only inherited wisdom. There was no curriculum, just many hours of sitting together, discussing the notes of a particular raga, why the sa was played the least—as a surprise element almost—in raga Marwa. Their breaks were nourished with bhajias and kokum chutney, a particular favourite of Khansahib.

Quite often, Vilayat Khan would say, 'Arvind, chalo. Enough for today. Let's go for a drive to Juhu beach and eat some bhel and bhutta.'

Or they would catch a movie in town; Vilayat loved the movies. After that, they went out for dinner, usually to a restaurant called Kit Kat, opposite Metro Cinema. But the restaurant served non-vegetarian food, which was strictly unpalatable for Arvind, so he would stroll around outside while his teacher finished his meal.

Vilayat Khan stood on the balcony of Ivorine, an art deco building along the Oval Maidan near Churchgate. He was a dashing twenty-two year old, and wore tinted sunglasses though the evening light was warm and mellow. Vilayat pulled out his red Craven 'A' box, lit a cigarette, took a deep drag, and stared into the distance at nothing in particular.

Boys in white played cricket on the green, their distant joyful shouts and the chorus of birds on their way home infused the evening with the feeling that the world is sometimes a good place. A long white Dodge glided past on the road below, and Vilayat Khan's eyes lit up momentarily, following it until it disappeared from sight. It was not the car he had been coveting, but it was still a beauty.

'Arvind,' he said to the student who stood behind him, trying to keep a distance from the smell of tobacco smoke without appearing disrespectful. 'I love this place. It's such a beautiful part of Bombay. You are lucky to live here. Look at those buildings. What beauty. That clock tower in front of us …' He pointed to the Rajabai Tower that loomed magnificently out of the palm trees. 'It reminds me of the Big Ben.'

Arvind looked quizzically at Vilayat with the patience that had become a necessary buffer in all their interactions, musical and non-musical. The young Khansahib started humming the tune of the Big Ben chimes. They were like a short question and answer, he said, moving his fingers as he sang.

'Da da da da … da da da da.'

He threw out his cigarette, shut his eyes and continued humming. Slowly, like a magical spell, the Big Ben tune started morphing into raga Hamsadhwani. He added another phrase, turned it around, played with it some more, and suddenly he was cradling a lovely composition, his fingers were already moving and tapping the balustrade, restless to transpose it on to the strings. He kept humming it, building on it as he walked back into the room, sat down, picked up his instrument and started playing it. Within minutes, it had crystallised into a beautiful piece of music. It was almost as if there was an invisible instrument playing inside him all the time.

Less than an hour earlier, Vilayat had told Arvind about his bus ride from Mohammed Ali Road to Churchgate. He sat, as he always did, upstairs in the open-deck bus, right in front, an excellent vantage point from which to view the city he had started to love. As the bus cruised through the streets of Bombay, he started singing a tune in raga Desh to himself—rather loudly at one point, for a Parsi lady behind him turned to the bus conductor and said, 'I think there is a mad man on our bus.'

The 'mad man' chuckled to himself. When it was time for him to get off, he stood up, walked past his crotchety co-passenger, then suddenly turned around, lurched at her and screamed 'boo'. She shrieked in fright. He laughed his way down the aisle and scampered off the bus.

An hour later, he was creating beauty. It was as if there were two different people inside the same blue kurta.

Arvind inwardly muttered a prayer of gratitude, suddenly feeling blessed. His teacher was this mercurial person, like Mozart was known to be, who could be so ridiculous and playful that you almost stopped taking him seriously and wondered whether this was a case of arrested development, and just then he would suddenly turn around and reveal unearthly genius.

This was what it was like most of the time. His whimsical

behaviour ranged from mild distractions—such as proclaiming after dinner, 'Come on, let's go for a drive to Lonavla,' ignoring feeble protests that it was eleven at night and the hill station was more than two hours away—to more naughty escapades which may have involved women, even married women.

The student was his antithesis—he was very conservative, very married and very sober. But Arvindbhai's Gujarati business acumen had already figured out that it was best to ignore the unwholesome aspects of his guru's personality and focus on the ones that would profit his life, the parts that were clearly bestowed with grace.

The relationship that would develop between them over the next sixty years was as unlikely and as uncommon as one between fire and water. But it was sustained by an interdependence between the practical and the lyrical. This friendship would also prove to be one of the abiding features in Vilayat Khan's chronically fractured life, filled with ephemeral commitments and short-lived relationships.

One afternoon in the early 1950s, Vilayat Khan was relaxing on the carpet with Arvindbhai in his Churchgate flat. Neither was in the mood for a lesson. The phone rang. It was Ali Akbar Khan, the sarod player who had become close to Vilayat Khan during their time together at AIR.

Arvindbhai handed the telephone to Khansahib, who listened and nodded at the receiver.

'Sure, sure, Alu-da, we have no plans. We will come. If you want us to come now to meet him, we can. We are not too far from there.'

Ali Akbar Khan was with his employer, Maharaja Hanwant Singh of Jodhpur, at the West End Hotel in New

Marine Lines. He had called to find out if Vilayat Khan was free that evening to play a private concert. The maharaja's friend, a nawab from Hyderabad, was throwing a party in Hanwant Singh's honour.

'Chalo, let's go make some money,' said Khansahib. 'We will meet Alu-da and also meet the maharaja. I believe he is here with his young wife, Zubeida.'

The two of them walked across to the hotel, past the red velvet furniture in the lobby to the grandest suite upstairs. The maharaja was standing, looking extremely stylish in Jodhpurs and a beige shirt. Zubeida sat on a chair near the window, wearing a powder-pink chiffon that was as enticing as a glass of champagne in the afternoon. Her wavy shoulder-length hair was conspicuously uncovered. Vilayat remembered hearing that she had shaken the royal family with her hold on the young prince. They chatted for a little while, then Ali Akbar and Vilayat Khan proceeded to the bar downstairs. Arvindbhai excused himself and said he would join them later.

That evening, they all went to the nawab's house. The porch sparkled with cut-glass chandeliers. A sarangi player and tabaliya were belting out a tune and Zubeida twirled to it. After some time, the nawab asked Vilayat Khan to play. He did, until he saw that the guests were bored and eager to move to the next round of entertainment.

He went and sat on the veranda and lit a cigarette. After a few minutes, he turned to Alu-da and whispered, 'Err ... there is going to be some money coming to us, no?'

'I have no idea, Vilayatbhai.'

They sat around a little longer, feeling a bit ignored. About half an hour later, the nawab called the three young men into his room. He opened an enormous Burma teak cupboard, and Vilayat Khan winked at Arvindbhai, expecting a healthy roll of notes.

To Vilayat's horror, the nawab reached into his cupboard and pulled out a sparkling dagger. The sheath was covered with the intricate bejewelled design that was famous in the nawab's home state. He handed it with both hands to Vilayat Khan.

'Thank you for your lovely music.'

Arvindbhai looked amused. As they walked out of the house, Vilayat lit a cigarette and said, 'What on earth does he think I am going to do with this?' He was livid. He couldn't stop cursing the nawab and all the others who had conned him into performing that evening.

A few days later, Hanwant Singh and Zubeida died in a plane crash. He had taken her up for a bird's-eye view of the Republic Day lights twinkling across Jodhpur.

By now, Vilayat Khan was performing fairly regularly and charged 150 rupees for a concert. This gradually went up to 500 rupees, then 750, and finally, by the 1950s, to 1,500 rupees. In those days, this was among the highest fees received by any performing musician.

Vilayat Khan's music had begun to soar, and so did his public profile as one of Bombay's top musicians. He was performing with the most robust accompanists of the time—Alla Rakha, Kishan Maharaj, Samta Prasad. Every big music conference in the country invited him—the Harivallabh Sangeet Sammelan in Jullunder, the All Bengal Music Conference in Calcutta, the Prayag Festival in Allahabad, the Shankarlal Festival in Delhi, the Haridas Sammelan in Bombay and Sawai Gandharva in Pune. He had a sizeable number of invitations from wealthy families to play private concerts in their living rooms.

In 1957, Vilayat was invited to play for the snobbish

Bombay Madrigal Singers Organisation, which otherwise featured Western classical music. The concert took place in the grand Cowasji Jehangir Hall in Fort. According to one newspaper, 'There was pin drop silence throughout, unlike the rustling and coughing one usually hears.'

In 1958, Bombay was treated to a glorious duet between Ali Akbar Khan and Vilayat Khan at Brabourne Stadium, near Marine Drive. There was great public enthusiasm over the event. Young and old showed up, partly to see and be seen. For Vilayat Khan was by then a celebrity. They played Yaman, Darbari and Bhairavi. One review noted that the two artistes, who were close friends, 'showed no desire to outwit each other'.

A couple of years later, Vilayat Khan played his first duet with Bismillah Khan at Shanmukhananda Hall, in the eastern suburbs of Bombay, where they were accompanied by Vilayat's old friend Ahmed Jan Thirakwa. Although he had always felt musically compromised playing duets, the shehnai master and he adored each other and their love showed through in the performances.

An abundance of critical acclaim started coming his way, and the reviews were filled with flattering, flowery adjectives. In 1958, the music critic of *The Times of India* wrote:

> Vilayat Khan, the sitar virtuoso, was in fine form when he gave a brilliant performance at the fifth session of the Haridas Sangeet Sammelan last night. His rendering of the Raga Yamani was notable for its technical mastery, bold and vigorous approach and a unique sanctity of notes. His musical diction was direct, clear and appealing ... The competent tabla accompaniment by Alla Rakha was ideal, correct and unobtrusive.

Music lovers still reminisce about that night under the stars at Rang Bhavan's open-air stage in the late fifties. Vilayat Khan came on last, after Bismillah Khan and Latafat Hussain Khan. That night, he sang a famous Abdul Karim Khan composition in raga Basant. The audience begged for more. He happily obliged them, playing Bhairavi. As a full moon rose above the trees, no one budged from their seats. Even the ushers seemed to turn into statues, mesmerised.

Bombay had turned into a lively city, abundant with money and enthusiasm. Vilayat Khan had a dedicated fan club of powerful people who patronised him, invited him for soirees, learned from him and lavished him with gifts. One such follower ran a popular antique shop at Chowpatty, called Solomon's Mines. In 1956, he decided to privately produce Vilayat Khan's record and launch what would become one of the first long playing records of the time. It had raga Rageshri on one side and raga Pilu on the other. Curiously, the album was dedicated to another musical nightingale who was rising to fame at the same speed as Vilayat. Her name was Lata Mangeshkar.

It was also in the fifties that Vilayat Khan started travelling abroad. In 1951, he was part of a cultural delegation to Britain, and among the first Indian musicians to perform there. From then on, there were regular concert tours to various international destinations—Russia, China, Afghanistan, Iran, and England and other parts of Europe.

But Vilayat Khan most loved those intimate private concerts filled with attentive, obsessive listeners. Sometime in the fifties, he and Alla Rakha played what would be their longest concert ever in Dharwad, the town in Karnataka that has spawned some of India's finest musicians. The concert was inside a school classroom, and there were no more than forty people in the audience. The two musicians played for eleven hours straight, with two short breaks. By the third segment, Vilayat Khan's fingers started bleeding, but he tied little strips of cloth on them and continued playing. There was a man in the first row who shouted 'wah wah' the loudest. He disappeared for a while in the middle, and when he returned, his exclamations were even louder. His name was Bhimsen Joshi.

Arvindbhai became not just Vilayat's student, but also his secretary and financial planner. He knew that money was like sand in his teacher's hands. Vilayat Khan had a strange relationship with wealth—he was charitable, profligate and stingy all at once. So, Arvind would play a little game with his teacher. He became the liaison between the master and the concert organisers. When they handed over a fee of, say 250 rupees, he told his teacher he was getting only 200. The rest he put aside in a parallel savings account for him. When it came to money matters, Vilayat Khan trusted Arvindbhai above himself.

Around this time, Arvindbhai started looking around for a suitable apartment in Bombay for his teacher. He finally found a pleasant one-bedroom flat in a building called Stardust, off Nepean Sea Road, near the Walsingham House School for girls, two minutes from the ocean. The only problem was that the building belonged to the maharaja of Kutch and his estate managers were reluctant to give it to a Muslim, that too a performing artiste. That meant two negatives, for this was a community known to be erratic and noisy, and the issue of food smells was also raised. It would compromise the respectability of the building.

Not one to be deterred, Arvindbhai found a relative who was closely associated with the Kutch royal estate, and persuaded him to prevail on the maharaja. He took full responsibility for the conduct of his teacher and explained that Vilayat Khan was not just some crude paan-chewing musician but a refined gentleman who wore suits and could dance the Viennese waltz. The deal came through—at a rent of 150 rupees per month. He would have preferred the flat next door with a balcony overlooking the ocean, but that was a full 100 rupees more, which his teacher would not have been able to afford.

The day the deal was closed, Vilayat Khan was returning from a music tour in China. Arvindbhai went to receive him at the airport. Vilayat emerged from the gates wearing a suit, dark glasses and a narrow-rimmed hat, looking like an Indian Clark Gable.

'I have found you the perfect flat, Khansahib,' Arvind said. He told him where it was and what the rent would be.

'Oh, but will I be able to afford that?'

'Of course you will, Khansahib. Now you are a star.'

Vilayat Khan's sitar was not an external prop; it had become an extension of his body, another limb. Even when he was not playing, he would constantly engage with his instrument, stare at it, fiddle with the ivory bridge, run his hand along the strings, pressing one down to see how the sound changed, strum downward and upward. He was his instrument, his instrument was him. This is why his fingers often moved even when he was not playing. His children and students would see his fingers move or tap while he was fast asleep. The music never stopped.

One morning, in the Stardust flat, probably sometime in the late 1950s, Vilayat Khan told his brother Imrat Khan to go to the other room. Khansahib had been experimenting with

Arvindbhai

the strings. He wanted Imrat to only hear the sound, not see what he was doing, because the visual input might colour his aural judgement.

For the next few hours, he kept tooling around with his instrument, what he called 'chhed-chhad', with no attention to time, the way a person might spend a morning chatting with a best friend, in a space of easy intimacy.

When he finally started playing, Imrat came to the door and said, 'Bhaiya! What did you just do? It sounds amazing!'

'Imrat! My brother! You won't believe what I have done. Look. I have just got rid of the pancham string. I don't know what's happening. Come here! Listen to this!' He jumped up, gave his younger brother an enormous hug and then proceeded to waltz around the room with him.

What had just happened was extraordinary. By retuning the two main strings, he had just irrevocably transformed the texture and tone of the sitar. Essentially, he had started fashioning the iconic 'gandhar pancham' sitar. The idea behind it was to have the raga's dominant notes completely available to the player of the instrument, so that they would reflect and resonate the notes of the raga being played and create a powerful musical atmosphere.

This also explains why the Vilayat Khan school of sitar players don't usually feel the need to use the tanpura as an accompanying background drone—because it allows the silent spaces between the notes to actually be silent. The reinvented sitar was able to create a new accoustic ambience. The player could make the instrument truly imitate the voice, with all its pauses and modulations.

A few months later, when Vilayat described these new ideas to Kanhai Lal, his father's old sitar-maker in Calcutta, the old man looked at him and said, '*Khoka, tor matha kharap hoye gyachhe ... Son, you are going crazy.*'

But Vilayat had aroused the curiosity of the seasoned instrument maker. The old man also knew that this particular khoka was not to be dismissed. He put aside one instrument to experiment with and started adding the elements requested by this brash young man whom he had known from the time he was a toddler.

A year or two later, when Vilayat Khan came to see him, he said, 'Vilayat, I've created this beast for you. Please take it away and do what you like with it. It's your baby now.' He could scarcely have known that he had created the first version of what would eventually become the industry standard.

Vilayat Khan continued to work tirelessly with the country's top instrument makers, Kanhai Lal and Hiren Roy in Calcutta, and later, Rikhi Ram in Delhi, to reconfigure the sitar. He later removed the brass pancham string and replaced it with a steel string. This dramatically changed the acoustic atmosphere around the intrument.

The six-string sitar was born.

He got rid of the second gourd, the one on top, which was earlier used for amplification, but after the introduction of microphones, served no purpose other than cosmetic. Then, he had the instrument makers reshape the gourd or tabli, giving it a slightly curved dome-like shape to create greater resonance. Vilayat was looking for a completely different tonal texture from the sitar. He also increased the curvature of the frets so that he could bend the notes far more: up to five notes. The human voice has a range of expression, and that is what he wanted to draw out from a sitar—bass to treble.

This new, neat version of the instrument eventually became the sitar standard across the country and even musicians from rival schools started demanding the 'Vilayatkhani sitar' from instrument makers.

Finally, Vilayat Khan ergonomically changed the position of the sitar to make it easier to handle, lifting it from its earlier position so that it was held at a 45-degree angle to the floor to reduce stress on the left arm. It is possible that this was also motivated by his profound sense of aesthetics.

These interventions enabled him to play his sitar with all the elements of a vocal performance: the slow meditative khayal, the faster taans, and the light thumri or dadra piece which most vocal musicians throw in like a delicate sorbet at the end of a four-course meal.

I could not quite enter the life of a man who had transformed his instrument without becoming intimate with it myself. For him, a line drawn across a piece of paper was never merely a line, it was a sitar string—something that could potentially change the universe.

I sat in the music room in Arvindbhai's elegant sea-facing home in Bombay for my first sitar lesson. It was the eve of Vilayat Khan's tenth death anniversary. He would have been eighty-six years old. The music room was the temple where devotees gathered every evening. The couch on which Vilayat Khan had sat and taught Arvindbhai for years was where the student now sat, offering the same wisdom, singing the same compositions, in that way that gulmohars blossom at the same time every year. New flowers, old tree. The students were different. The music was the same.

Instruments of varied vintage and size stood against the wall in different corners of the room. Arvindbhai handed me a beautiful sitar, a slim one, smaller than the one he played. An orange and green thread was tied around the upper half of its stem. The ivory inlay work looked vaguely ancient.

'I picked this one up from Khansahib many years ago for 600 rupees. It is from the Enayat Khan collection. It had been left in his home by some zamindar who had beome penniless and was forced to sell off all his things.'

I was reminded of my first day in another music room with my beloved teacher Dhondutai, where I sat as a reluctant student, oblivious to how that day would change my life. Arvindbhai appointed one of his senior students, Deepak Raja, a musicologist and an obsessive Vilayat Khan fan, to teach me. Deepak gently pushed the mizrab or plucker on to the tip of my right index finger. I winced, for it was too tight. It is said that when Enayat Khan died, his students fought over his mizrab.

I was not expected to do much more than get my posture right. Straight back. Sitar at a precise 45-degree angle from the body, the round tumba resting in the crook of my knee. I went through the frets, all seven notes, up once and down once. Press with your left index finger until you reach the last note. Play this with the next finger. This is enough for today, Deepak said.

Arvindbhai told me about the time he had started accompanying his teacher at concerts. In the early days, during a programme at Laxmi Baug, Vilayat Khan played for almost five hours without giving Arvindbhai the chance to play. On their way back, at three in the morning, he asked his teacher why he had been punished thus.

'Arre, Arvind, first at least learn to sit on the stage for five hours non-stop with the sitar in your hands. That itself takes enormous mental and physical stamina,' he said. 'Then let's move to the next step.'

There were no shortcuts in this world. You could not hurry. You had to first sit. Sit and wait. Sit and wait with complete faith. And slowly, slowly, the world opened itself up to you. Then, there was no going back.

SIR SHANKAR LAL MUSIC FESTIVAL

AT LYTTON ROAD — NEAR RABINDRA BHAWAN

Daily From 6-30 P.M. onwards

4th MARCH

Girja Devi	Vocal
Bismillah Khan	Shahnai
Nasir Amin Uddin Dagar	Vocal
Ali Akbar Khan	Sarod
Samta Parshad	Tabla

5th MARCH

Sharan Rani	Sarod
Mishra Bandhu	Vocal
Vilayat Khan	Sitar
Imrat Khan	Surbahar
Samta Parshad	Tabla

Rates Rs. 5/- (Reserved)
Rs. 2/- per day

Available at Cottage Industries Emporium, Janpath, and Lahore Music House, Daryaganj.

You are requested to be in your seats by 6-25 P.M.

The gates will close at 6-30 P.M. sharp.

(99049)

CHAPTER FIVE

The Music

At some point in his life, if he is lucky, an artist moves from being a technically competent master to a creative spirit. Most musicians fall somewhere along that spectrum. Very few stay consistently brilliant. Some may achieve that sublime space only at a particular moment in their performing life; some may reach it in private, and no one would even know. Some practice and practice but only start flying in another lifetime; a few reach it only as teachers, not performers. But no one can explain how the shift takes place. It has so much to do with destiny. It has so little to do with fame.

In Vilayat Khan's life, there came a time when years of stubborn determination and monastic practice yielded to a space of ease. He now held his instrument without the desire to dominate it; the mind and body and the sitar were able to interact in a space of love. Something else began to happen.

The period between 1960 and 1985 were perhaps Vilayat Khan's best musical years. This was when his music elicited the 'aah' of true wonder and gratitude, not merely the 'wah' that comes with applause. His technique perfected, he had soared into a realm of imagination and creativity.

And yet, his experimenting was in no way gratuitious. There was a strong respect for tradition and a deep recognition of the integrity of the raga, but within that he had the guts to introduce a kind of radical modernity, the kind that comes when a person is so confident in his tradition that he is able to make those little flights into something new and occasionally bring out the hidden dragon.

He achieved this modern element by playing with timbre and volume to create effects that were nothing short of revolutionary. While other sitar players used the strings for melody, Vilayat Khan was actually creating harmony. In fact, if you listened closely, you could sometimes hear an entire orchestra emerge from his sitar. There were always percussive elements, you could also hear the moaning of wind instruments, the staccato of piano, the emotional quality of the voice … all this overlaying and interplaying with the plucking and strumming.

This was also the period when Vilayat Khan transcended extraordinary stroke-craft and cajoled the sitar into sounding like the human voice. It really was a master-move because of the depth of emotion this brought to the music.

Vocal music has always had primacy in Indian classical music. However perfectly strings may be tuned, an instrument may not have the same impact on a listener as the sound that comes from the same place as breath. An instrument is a prop that is outside the self and therefore cannot produce the finest, most subtle vibrations that the voice is capable of. An inherently powerful instrument, the human voice is the first medium of communication used by a newborn. It is what a mother uses to comfort her child. The voice is directly connected with breath, with the life force.

By bringing his instrument so close to the voice, Vilayat Khan elevated the place of the sitar in the caste system of singers and instrumentalists. His 'gayaki anga' (vocalist style) was a significant departure from the 'tantkar anga' (the style that describes plucked instruments). The crucial difference between vocal music and a plucked instrument is that vocal music is able to establish continuity, while the frets of an instrument create a staccato effect. Vilayat Khan could effectively play with what is known as 'meend', the indiscernible continuum of notes between two notes, which only a singer can achieve. He had both the craft and the knowledge to fill the space in between. And the audience was lapping it up.

He also knew how to get the best out of the microphone to vary timbre, tone and volume, and to elicit the reverberation of the sustained note. By placing the microphone at precise points in front of and behind his instrument, he could produce the shehnai effect, the sitar effect, replicate the piano, even the tabla. Without the advantage of amplification and sophisticated acoustics, his predecessors had to focus on force rather than these nuances.

Deepak Raja explains it best in one of his essays: 'He enabled the experience of sitar music to transcend the limitations of the technology of the instrument and brought it closer to the acoustic, aesthetic and emotional richness of vocal music ... A crucial limitation the sitar has—in relation to the human voice—is the communication of emotional values. The human voice communicates them effectively with the aid of variations in volume and timbre. In his attempts at singing on the sitar, Vilayat Khan evolved an entire science of acoustics for manipulation of these variables on the sitar.'

The public began to recognise and acknowledge this incredible new element in sitar music. In 1956, an article in *The Times of India* said:

> Vilayat Khan has launched a bold experiment with his gayaki style. Like a ventriloquist who appears to speak through the dummy in his hand, so Vilayat Khan sings through the sitar, imitating the most difficult inflections of vocal music on the instrument.

Although Vilayat Khan had promised his mother he would not sing, he found a way out by smuggling his singing into virtually every concert. It was an audacious manoeuvre. His voice became the signature feature of a Vilayat Khan performance. No sitar player had dared to do this. Boundaries were being broken.

On rare occasions, the powerful vocalist in him would really let go. At a private concert in the home of a friend in Calcutta, he announced that he would only sing that evening. The friend knew this was a rare moment and asked his permission to record the music. Over the next three hours, Vilayat Khan presented extraordinary renditions, including three variations of raga Khat. He sang Shri, Darbari Kanada and Chhaya Nat.

A few days after the concert, Vilayat Khan asked the host for the cassette, saying that he would like to listen to it. The friend sent it across.

That was the last he ever saw of it. A few months later, when he meekly asked for the tape back, Khansahib looked at him with great surprise and said, 'What tape?'

In his autobiography *Komal Gandhar*, written in Bengali and compiled by Shankarlal Bhattacharya, Vilayat Khan says that his 1962 recording of Tilak Kamod reveals all the changes that he had incorporated into the sitar—where his temperament, the instrument and beauty all came together to create what he describes as 'the ultimate Vilayat Khansahib'.

I went across to Deepak Raja's house to listen to the Tilak Kamod. I had given up as a student of the sitar, but was still trying to learn this music the next best way—by listening mindfully. I had to do this with someone who had analysed and adored it for years.

We sat in his music room, a progeny of many music rooms, both known and unknown. Over the years, Deepak had built up an enviable collection of recordings through many exchanges with other music-obsessed collectors. The provenance of many of these pieces remains blurry, or anonymous, or secret, for that is the way collectors operate.

'Just listen to this one first,' he said.

It was a Bhairavi played in 1976 at the Bhulabhai Auditorium in Bombay, the first acoustically designed concert hall in the city. Vilayat Khan was playing the sitar at a memorial concert for his old mentor Ahmed Jan Thirakwa. The tabla master had just passed away and, like many unlettered artistes, had not bothered with matters quotidian like savings and bank accounts. Now his granddaughter was getting married and the family needed to raise money. Vilayat Khan jumped in to help. Khansahib spoke about his love for Thirakwa and then struck the half notes of raga Bhairavi, instantly transporting his audience into a courtesan's chambers in medieval Lucknow. He had selected a well-known thumri, sung over the decades by many: 'Baat Chalat Nayi Chunari Rang Daari'. Vilayat Khan played and sang intermittently.

The recording was so perfect, it felt as if we were there. We could visualise a kathak dancer move, hear the ghungroo bells tinkle, smell a whiff of the mogra attar. When Mohammed Ahmed Khan began the tabla accompaniment, we could almost see Khansahib smile and tap his feet under his shawl.

Halfway through the raga, Vilayat Khan suddenly changed his scale and played the same notes on a scale half a note lower. It was a genius move which he often pulled off, suddenly surprising the audience, making them sit up just in case they had been lulled into a happy stupor.

'I am hearing singing,' said Deepak. 'There is very little stroke work here, the sitar is singing. It puts you in a totally different zone. Singing removes all barriers of communication, instrumental music is still mechanical. So he will be singing away with his sitar, and then suddenly he will throw you a googly with a piece demonstrating brilliant instrumental technique to say, "Don't forget this is Vilayat Khan playing" … It's like Bhimsen Joshi. He could be singing a simple devotional abhang … and then suddenly he would pull out a scintillating taan to remind you that he was Bhimsen Joshi.

'All great musicians and composers have the uncanny ability to know exactly when the listener needs relief, a sudden change in pace, that element of surprise,' said Deepak. 'Vilayat Khan, Beethoven, Mozart, they all knew. After a particularly dense segment, Vilayat Khan would inevitably throw in a light lilting phrase. You can see it in his ragamalas.'

After this, Deepak played the stunning Tilak Kamod that I had gone there to hear. An hour later, after the last note had been struck, we sat in silence.

Several minutes later, I said, 'There is a particular word that comes to mind right now. Thehrav. Can you translate it into English, Deepak?'

Deepak smiled because he knew exactly what I was talking

about—it was precisely what was missing in the music of so many young sitar players today. It was the stillness, that meditative, unhurried space.

'How about leisurely deliberation ... A space that involves both introspection and expression, a simultaneous movement inward and outward.'

'Serene deliberation?' I said. 'That long pause we all crave. Not just in music, but in the way we live.'

He reached out and picked up an Urdu-to-English dictonary, but of course there was nothing that came close to the word 'thehrav'. Some things are better left unexplained.

I wondered why I loved Vilayat Khan's music so much and why I could listen to it for hours, despite my short attention span issues. What resonated with me was the way his music brought together tradition and rebellion. We exist in an intricate web of past moments, present expression and future possibilities and his art seemed to contain it all in a seamless way, reminding us of that continuum.

CHAPTER SIX

Portrait of a Young Musician

Vilayat Khan was a man of average height and incredible good looks. He was fair, with a broad forehead, a large aquiline nose and thick robust lips. He wore rimless and, later, steel-rimmed spectacles.

As a young man, he was a magnificent narcissist, always conscious of the way he looked and how he came across to the world. Also, he cultivated a public persona quite distinct from his real self, which only his family and close friends were privy to. He mastered a slow, deliberate style of speech, which was invariably filled with liberal embellishment of facts. His storytelling, mimicry and jokes made him hugely popular with people young and old. One of his relatives remembers how Vilayat Khan was chatting away at home one day, until suddenly a guest was at the door, and Khansahib changed his kurta as well as his speaking style. Clark Kent became Superman.

Even when he was impoverished, Vilayat Khan had been obsessed with wearing smart clothes and enjoyed seeing himself featured in newspapers and magazines as a flamboyant musician. This is why, though he enjoyed them thoroughly, he smoked beedis only in private and cigarettes and pipes in public. He carefully curated his appearance on stage, from precisely when he would enter to the manner in which he covered his feet with a shawl. That was his rock star side, but it was all within traditional trappings, which is what made it unique.

'Arvind, *mere khate mein* total *kitna hai*? How much have you collected for me?' he asked his student one day.

'Khansahib, I will tell you only if you tell me why you want to know,' Arvindbhai replied with a cheeky smile.

'You will get cross if I tell you, but I want 300 rupees. *Baat aisi hai ki* ...' He had ordered a suit at a tailor shop but had not been able to collect it because he couldn't pay up.

Another day, he asked a friend to help him procure a dressing table.

'Khansahib, it is very expensive, but why don't we improvise the way my mother once did?'

He asked how, and the friend explained that she had bought two wooden crates, covered them with an embroidered sheet, and placed a framed mirror on top of it. It became a perfectly presentable dressing table.

'Very good idea. Let's do it!'

They organised the chests and put the pieces together, and soon after that, Vilayat Khan was standing in front of the mirror in his new suit, preening like a peacock, turning his head this way and that. He grimaced slightly and said, 'Everything else is fine but I think *ek jagah maar khaya*—I was short-changed on one thing—height!'

Five young men lay around languidly in the vast living room of Naushad Ali's sea-facing bungalow in Bandra, staring at the ceiling fan which turned grumpily. A massive tiger skin was stretched across one of the walls. It was a humid May afternoon, but a gentle breeze lapped around them and tempered the heat.

'You know, my father always taught me that the ultimate aim of the musician is not to develop technical mastery, but a pure and tender heart ...' Ali Akbar Khan said with great earnestness. Lying on the carpet next to him were Vilayat Khan, Naushad, Madan Mohan and his brother Prakash.

'Then why do you keep giving it away to a woman, Alu-da? She will only demolish it, and you will be left with no heart and no music,' said Madan Mohan, and the others chuckled.

During his long stay in Bombay, Vilayat Khan became very close to Madan Mohan and Naushad, two of the Hindi film industry's most highly regarded music composers. They used to spend hours together in one of their homes, or at Arvindbhai's Churchgate flat, or strolling on the Marine Drive promenade, discussing music, drinking, dreaming. Whenever he was visiting from Jodhpur, Ali Akbar Khan would also join them.

It is likely that many film tunes came out of these interactions. Naushad's compositions were filled with ragas. Madan Mohan was known to be a friendly thief of catchy tunes. His propensity to casually lift riffs from here and there had long been a joke in the industry, and people used to say, 'Protect your tunes, Madi is coming!'

There are many colourful tales about the origins of Madan Mohan's memorable song *Mera Saya*, which went on to haunt the nation. In one story, Vilayat Khan was giving a private concert at his student Prabhuddha Bhagat's home in Khar and Madan Mohan was sitting in the front row, swaying to the music. He asked his buddy to play raga Nand. Every time he played the signature phrase, Madi applauded and burped a slurry 'wah'. A few months later, the same tune found its way into the song *Mera Saya*. Vilayat Khan's touch, and even his sitar, can be heard in the music of films like *Madhosh* and *Dekh Kabira Roya*. But notions of plagiarism did not afflict an artiste like Vilayat Khan who had himself been a hunter-gatherer of music and built his repertoire with help from the recordings of past masters. Besides, it is possible that he was so well established as a classical artiste that he didn't really care about getting credit in the film world. It was his nephew Rais Khan who played regularly for Madan Mohan movies.

By the 1950s, popular Hindi cinema had turned into a formidable force and film music became India's ambient soundtrack. Not surprisingly, many classical artistes working in radio stations gravitated towards it. Like radio, cinema had created a new national narrative, cutting across language and region, and offered a tempting new source of income for classical musicians. In the new post-feudal India, they also realised the need to cultivate a national audience.

Film studios became playgrounds for some of the most talented music directors of all time. Hindi film music grew out of a confluence of the Bengal stream, the Marathi stream and Western music, which came from Anglo-Indians and later Goans. The Bengal stream came from Calcutta, where composers like Pankaj Mullick and R.C. Boral had been working in New Theatres studio, and had made some bold experiments fusing elements of Western harmony and orchestra with traditional Indian classical music. Mullick was influenced by Rabindra Sangeet, and Boral was a well-established tabla player who was close to Enayat Khan and had even accompanied him on several concerts. The Marathi stream, which was the more dominant one initially, came out of Pune and Kolhapur, and had much more of a Hindustani classical element, thanks to playback artistes like Saraswati Devi, a Parsi dhrupad singer who worked for Bombay Talkies. When Bengali composers like Anil Biswas migrated to the thriving Bombay industry, they started changing the music scene, eliminating the Marathi elements, bringing in other melodies, introducing Western instruments.

The confluence of all these new sounds reflected the unique cosmopolitan energy of Bombay. The backbone of film music, where the different strains came together, was the orchestra. This was a new and wonderfully democratic space where a saxophonist from Goa could be sitting next to a sitar player from Banaras. An uppity fourth-generation classical artiste was no different from the nutty bongo player; they all had to show up on time at Famous Studios or Mehboob Studios or Bombay Labs for the morning shift, where a single microphone, or maybe two, would unite them. Whatever their individual talent might be, they had to respect one another, integrate, hold back when the other played, and conform to the demands of the footage and the director's very specific requirements. And, worse, they had to rehearse before the bigger star—the playback singer—showed up.

Not surprisingly, many classical musicians were ambivalent about this new world. While they harboured contempt for popular music—perhaps a mask for some degree of insecurity—they also wanted to be part of a national obsession which was drowning out all other forms of entertainment. One hit song meant instant stardom, a lot of money, and photographs in glamorous magazines. So they all crawled in, reluctant maestros, seeking a bit of fame in a space that was veering towards easy listening thanks to the formidable force of broadcast technologies.

Some of them worked under pseudonyms. For example, in the 1940s, a talented Punjabi percussionist called A.R. Qureshi left his post in All India Radio in Bombay to work full-time for Rangmahal Studios, where he spent at least fifteen years as music director and composed music for at least thirty films (including *Bewafa*, *Khandaan* and *Alam Ara*), working with major directors like Naushad and Avinash Vyas. But when this tabla master wore his classical hat and accompanied Ravi Shankar or Vilayat Khan on stage, he was Alla Rakha, the classical tabla ustad, who later became even more famous as the father of Zakir Hussain. Because of the miserable way he was treated in the film industry—made to wait for hours on end, not paid on time—he finally left it in 1958 and focused exclusively on classical music. This was the time when he did some breathtaking recordings and foreign concert tours with Ravi Shankar.

So, while their names may not feature on the credits, they all played for cinema: Ali Akbar Khan, Halim Jaffer Khan, Ram Narain, Alla Rakha, Ravi Shankar, Pannalal Ghosh, Amir Khan and, of course, Vilayat Khan, who had already been active in New Theatres in Calcutta. The entire background score of *Pakeezah* had Rais Khan on the sitar. Later, Hariprasad Chaurasia and Shivkumar Sharma joined the scene. At the time, many of these musicians were employed by All India Radio, which graciously allowed them to play on the side for film music.

But they continued to try and differentiate themselves from the other orchestra musicians whom they considered beneath them, often behaving badly or overplaying where they shouldn't. And the person who managed and manoeuvred these diverse personalities would be the music director—caressing egos, maintaining discipline and drawing out the best to craft some eternally memorable melodies.

When the music director Vasant Desai asked Bismillah Khan to play for *Goonj Uthi Shehnai* in 1958, the shehnai player strolled into the studio and rudely asked, 'What do you want me to do?' Desai saw that this attitude was not going to work. So he quietly said, 'Today, because of the heavy rain, we won't be able to get the best sound, so let's postpone the rehearsal to tomorrow.' They both knew he was lying. The next day, a suitably chastened Bismillah showed up and said gently, 'Vasantrao, tell me what I should play ...' and then proceeded to blow into his instrument to produce some beautiful music, including the sweet love song, 'Tere Sur Aur Mere Geet'. Some composers were not as charitable, though. A well-known sarangi player decided to go beyond his required three minutes to show off his virtuosity and was peremptorily stopped by the director with 'Play as much as you have been told'. No matter how talented the musician—whether he was a classical artiste or playback singer—he was completely dependent on the music director.

The music directors who managed to get around extreme behaviours and fragile egos often produced classics, making the trouble worth it. The great musical duo Shankar–Jaikishan used a galaxy of great artistes in their 1956 film *Basant Bahar*—Pannalal Ghosh on the flute, Ram Narain on sarangi and Bhimsen Joshi on vocals. Shankar–Jaikishan, who were more in tune with the classical space, composed the beautiful duet, 'Ketaki Gulab Juhi', a song in which two musicians, Tansen and Baiju Bawra, are competing before Emperor Akbar. Bhimsen Joshi had to sing with Manna Dey and then lose to him. Before they started out, Manna Dey was petrified about singing with such a great artiste, and even ran away from Bombay briefly; ironically, Bhimsen was equally nervous about losing his reputation as a classical singer. They both turned to Shankar Singh, the older of the duo, to show them the way and eventually produced a liltingly beautiful song.

Given his natural attraction to glamour, Vilayat Khan strolled into the Bombay film world with ease. He was often seen at Mehboob Studios in Bandra, alighting from his convertible, dark glasses on, a cigarette in one hand and his paan box in the other. He said, in a magazine interview, 'In Bombay, I was a playboy, like a film star. I used to dress like a film star, wearing French shirts adorned with red stripes and stars, as I drove around town in my two-seater Jaguar. I was very happy because of my playboy looks, and not my sitar playing. Nowadays this is very common for artistes. But then, musicians were known through their art. I became famous for my looks and image ... But sitar was never far from me; sitar has always been my body and soul.'

He initially latched on to his first cousin, Babbu or Khan Mastana, who was about ten years older than him. Khan Mastana had relinquished the classical sitar and his hereditary baggage, and gone on to become a playback singer and composer in the Bombay film world, much to the family's disdain. Of course, the family was less disapproving of his choices after he had a blockbuster hit in the movie *Shaheed*, 'Watan ki Raah Mein', and came into a fairly large amount of money as well as a couple of flats in Bombay. When Vilayat Khan moved to Bombay, an addled and unravelling Khan Mastana was called upon to teach Imrat Khan in his few sober moments.

Vilayat did play for a few films, but did not bother with taking formal credit for them.

In 1958, Satyajit Ray, perhaps India's most iconic film director, asked Vilayat Khan to compose the background score for *Jalsaghar*. Vilayat created a masterpiece, texturing the dark and light moods of the film with music. He was assisted by his brother Imrat Khan and used his uncle Wahid Khan on the surbahar; the sombre, almost melancholic bass sitar conjured up the heavy atmosphere surrounding an aristocrat unravelling in slow motion. Vilayat used music to change moods in a film that otherwise takes place largely in one setting. He used his influence to bring in the top artistes of the time—among them, Begum Akhtar and Bismillah Khan. Ray had earlier worked with Ravi Shankar on the *Apu Trilogy*. Both the trilogy and *Jalsaghar* had haunting musical narratives, but there had clearly been hiccups. Many years later, in an interview, Ray told the journalist Raju Bharatan, 'I can't deal with these classical musicians. The Goans and the film musicians play exactly what I want. They know how to play for the footage.'

In 1969, Vilayat Khan was invited by the international director duo Merchant–Ivory to direct the music for their film *Guru* about a British rock star (played by Michael York) who leaves a successful career in Britain to come to India and learn sitar from a master, played by the actor Utpal Dutt.

The last film he worked on was in 1975. He was the music director for *Kadambari*, starring Shabana Azmi. In one of the songs, 'Ambar ki Ek Pak Surahi', he used lyrics by the Punjabi poet Amrita Pritam and the voice of Asha Bhonsle.

Over the years, a spectrum of musicians—from chorus girls to classical artistes—embellished the film industry. Many were oblivious to their own potential. Some of the most extraordinarily talented ones remained orchestra artistes only because they didn't have the ambition or savvy to break out on their own or fight for individual credit.

People still remember Vilayat Khan's brother-in-law and close friend, Mohammed Shafi, Zeenat's second husband after her estrangement from Amir Khan. Shafi was considered a prodigy both as a sitar player and a composer. He was so talented that Naushad sent him to Russia to learn Western classical music. Shafi became extremely successful and bought several properties in Mahim. He was also known for his incredible generosity. But the man with the long white beard lived in the low key. He remained an assistant to Naushad until the end, largely unknown to the public.

In 1952, Amir Khan sang for Naushad's *Baiju Bawra* along with the other great singer D.V. Paluskar. The film about Tansen and Baiju, both students of Haridas Swami, became iconic. Vilayat Khan begged Naushad to let him sing for one of his films, but the great composer refused. He knew his friend well. If he indulged this vanity and let Vilayat do a playback song, his own films would benefit, but he could be contributing to the death of one of India's greatest sitar players.

'Vilayat miyan, when you pick up your sitar, all the ragas and raginis of the universe stand before you and say, "which one of us are you going to honour today?" I would be an enemy of music if I came in the way of such beauty. No, I will not let you sing for the movies even if it is my loss,' he said.

Many years later, Naushad was walking to the Haji Ali dargah on the path that cuts through the Arabian Sea, humming a song in raga Malkauns, 'Man Tarpat Hari Darshan ko Aaj'. When he was almost at the marble steps, he heard a familiar voice.

'*O garib nawaz, kadar kariye* ... Naushad saab, pass something to this poor man.'

He looked down and was shocked to see that it was a bedraggled Khan Mastana. The great Imdad Khan's grandson was begging for a living. Naushad gently helped him up, hugged him and took him home for a hot meal.

Not everyone had the luck of a Vilayat Khan.

The years in Bombay were heady times for the young musician. In the late 1940s, Vilayat made friends with a young man called Khalid Gaya, and together they would go for dance lessons to an Anglo-Indian dance academy on Grant Road. One afternoon, while working on their foxtrot, they came up with a business plan. They decided to rent a room in that area and employ two tailor masters. This would also be the space where Vilayat could practise undisturbed when the tailors were not working. He would spread a white sheet and sit on it for hours with his instrument, playing until his fingers bled, scarlet raindrops on snow.

When he was not practising music or teaching, the hubris of youth took over. There was always a woman in his life—and never for very long. The sitar was the spinal cord that kept him in alignment.

His first love was a woman called Suraiya, until he discovered that the bewitching young thing had cuckolded a close friend (whom he called Mohammed Rassiwala in an interview to protect his real identity). He initially refused to believe this unpleasant detail about his beloved. To prove it, Rassiwala orchestrated a sting operation in a Churchgate hotel, where he hid inside a wardrobe while Vilayat Khan confronted his lady love. At just the moment when she feigned complete ignorance, Rassiwala sprang out of the closet. The love affair ended right there.

Vilayat Khan often hung around with the actresses and chorus girls who dotted the world of Hindi cinema, and sometimes embarked on amorous expeditions. He became especially close to a singer and composer from Lucknow called Chandbala. It is said that Lata Mangeshkar used to go to her to improve her Urdu pronunciation. Although her talent and beauty were inversely proportional, Chandbala had a way with men.

Vilayat Khan must have been in his early twenties, Chandbala around the same age. They even got engaged to be married. But clearly he was not quite done with bachelorhood. While driving to a concert at Laxmi Baug one night, he confided his dilemma to a friend who sat in the driver's seat next to him.

'Tonight, after the programme, she will be in the car with us. I think you should break the news to her.'

'Me? Why me? How can I do your hatchet job months before your nikah has been scheduled?' the friend said. 'Amma has already given me an earful about her being a whore and all, but you've gone and got stuck deep in this one.'

'You have to, that's all,' said Vilayat.

So, later that night, after an exhilarating performance of Bihag and Yaman, the two of them were driving Chandbala home. On the way, they took a short detour and went to their favourite paan shops at Babulnath, which Vilayat Khan had nicknamed Chakoo and Chhuri. Vilayat Khan got out of the car to smoke a cigarette. Leaning on the bonnet of his car, he whispered to his friend, 'Do it now.'

They got back inside and once the car was cruising along, the friend glanced at Chandbala, who was in the back seat, combing her long curly hair and peering into the mirror in front.

'Bhabhi, I don't think you should go ahead with this marriage,' said the friend, without turning around, his eyes tightly shut, as if he anticipated a blow on the head from behind.

'What exactly do you mean,' she said, sharply.

'Well, Amma is totally against it, so you won't be happy and the home won't be peaceful, trust me.'

'What is this man saying? Janu, please tell him he's talking rubbish!'

'No, Chandbala, he's probably right,' said Vilayat, without looking back.

'What?' she shrieked. The friend shuddered. The evening was going downhill faster than the speedy taan that Vilayat Khan had just played to a standing ovation.

'Are you aware the cards have been printed and sent to half the film fraternity?' Her voice had grown louder and more shrill. 'My hands are covered in henna. What are you talking about? How humiliating this is. What do you mean by doing this to me, you sala bhadua. Motherfucker. I always knew you were a piece of dirty ass.' The abuses became more and more colourful.

She made Vilayat Khan stop the car and got out somewhere near Haji Ali. As she slammed the door shut and they drove on, Vilayat Khan turned to his friend and smiled wickedly.

'Allah miyan, that was a close call.'

It was a turning point. Chandbala took her revenge by seducing Vilayat Khan's nephew Rais Khan, who was then not quite out of his teens and turning into a brilliant sitar player, with looks and charm to match those of his uncle. He had learned from his father Mohammed Khan as well as from Vilayat Khan, who had stayed in their Babulnath home in his early days in Bombay.

Chandbala managed to get Rais Khan to not only fall in love with her, but also elope and marry her—a woman ten years his senior. The family cut off ties with him. Rais Khan moved into her Churchgate flat near the Astoria Hotel to live with her and her mother. And Chandbala vindicated herself by spending the next few years firing up the young and restless Rais against Vilayat Khan, persuading him that he was as good as his uncle and that he should declare it publicly.

This pointless competition between uncle and nephew

reached its climax sometime in 1965 at the Birla Matoshri Hall in Marine Lines. It was a trio performance by Vilayat, his brother Imrat and their nephew Rais. Chandbala had primed Rais Khan to outdo his uncle. The twenty-four-year-old played his instrument with maniacal zeal.

In the middle of the concert, the Kathak dancer Sitara Devi sprinkled more inflammable condiments into the frying pan. She stood up and said, 'Vilayat, why have you trapped these two youngsters? Why are you suppressing them? Let them shine forth.'

'Bilkul, bilkul! Of course! Both these kaccha bacchas are my students,' he replied, equally quick on the uptake.

The concert is still discussed in musical circles. Rais Khan continued to play brilliantly and was considered the only sitar player who could match Vilayat Khan. But he publicly declared that he had nothing to do with his uncle. He distanced himself from the family and eventually moved, two wives later, to Karachi in Pakistan.

Meanwhile, Vilayat Khan did not need long to move on to his next target, making Basheeran Begum crotchety and suspicious again.

'Who is this girl he has got involved with now?' she muttered to the bemused Imrat. 'What is wrong with your brother? If he wants to have many friends, it's fine. Why should he get into all this marriage chakkar?'

She was a fiercely controlling mother. Besides, her elder son was now also the family's established breadwinner, and had to be protected from predatory wives. This time, he had got involved with a pretty girl in Bhopal, the daughter of a land surveyor. To everyone's shock, he announced that he was engaged to be married to her.

When Amma heard about it, she was so irritated that, as a congratulatory gesture, she sent the girl's family sweet batasha indifferently wrapped in torn bits of sari, clearly displaying her feelings about the betrothal.

The girl's mother was livid at this insult. 'We have just celebrated a kabutar–kabutari marriage here. Even the pigeons were treated with more respect than this, Baba. What is this kind of behaviour? Who do these people think they are?'

But the marriage didn't break up on those grounds. Rather, a few months later, Vilayat himself grew nervous and had urgent second thoughts. In a roundabout move to break the relationship, he went to the girl's father and asked for 10,000 rupees in dowry, something he knew would be absolutely impossible for the family to organise. From here on, the situation degenerated to something like rancid butter.

The seething father knew what this self-centred man was up to, but there was nothing he could do. His daughter's honour was now at stake.

'Don't worry, I will try and arrange the money from somewhere, but I also have a condition in return,' he said to Vilayat Khan, not hiding his contempt. 'I will lay the notes on the floor, and you must walk on them from the door into the room.'

Eventually, Vilayat Khan left Bhopal. Single. As he boarded the train to leave, the girl's brother came to the compartment, imploring him to reconsider his decision, crouching on the floor and clutching his leg. Khansahib sat unmoved. The train whistle blew. The concert was over and the curtains had come down. No one knows what happened to the girl, but there were whispers that it was not a pleasant ending.

There was also a tall brunette—a German soprano married to a flautist. Her husband was posted in Bombay to oversee a prestigious cultural organisation. She was smitten by the sitar maestro, and even considered divorce at one point so that she could be with him. The relationship carried on for a couple of years until the husband protested and sent a message to Vilayat Khan that he had gone too far. Khansahib was scarcely deterred. He remarked casually to a friend with a laugh, 'Tell him to keep sucking on his sugarcane stick.'

And so, the women fluttered in and out of his life like beautiful, wounded butterflies. Sometimes he was the heart-breaker, at other times, he had his broken—like an encounter he supposedly had with a beguiling young film actress known for her lovely black ringlets. She was the daughter of a reputed courtesan singer who herself had a prolific and colourful personal life—she allegedly had four children from four different men.

It was the early 1950s. The young Khansahib, then in his early twenties, had just returned from a tour in London, and was on the verge of proposing to this girl. But Basheeran Begum put her foot down.

'All this time, I have only given you advice. This time I am instructing you,' she said in that severe tone reserved for only a few things—music and money, mostly. 'You cannot marry this whore, my son. She is the daughter of a singing girl, you come from a proper khandani family of classical musicians.'

'What do you mean? I love and adore her. You can't play around with a young man's feelings like this. Fine, Amma, if I can't marry her, I will stay unmarried for the rest of my life.'

'Well, son, there is a reason I am passing this order. It's a very big reason.'

That night, around midnight, not being able to sleep, Vilayat Khan went to his mother and asked her why she was intent on breaking his heart.

Basheeran Begum looked at him coldly and said, 'Because this girl is your sister.'

He was stunned. 'Amma, what are you saying?'

'Look at her features carefully, her eyes, her nose and her teeth and you will understand what I am saying.'

'I still don't believe you. What proof do you have that we are brother and sister?'

'You want proof? I will give you that too … now go to sleep.' And that was that.

The next morning, she said to Vilayat Khan, 'Take out the car, let's go there.'

'Where, Amma?'

'To her house.'

'But why? What is all this?'

'I will not stop now. I have to give you proof,' she said, pulling her head scarf over her head as she slipped into the front seat.

When they reached the flat on Marine Drive, the girl's mother was in her living room, sitting cross-legged and sipping tea. She was shocked to see them. She jumped up.

'Begum Sahiba? You here?'

'Yes, sister. I have come to your home. With Allah as witness, I must speak now …'

The girl's mother kept begging Amma to sit, but she insisted on standing. She finally relented and sat down. With a deep sigh, she said, 'Please tell this boy. Please tell him that your daughter's father is Enayat Khan. Your word is my only proof.'

The woman sat in silence, a mask creeping over her countenance which had clearly grown used to disguising emotion. Vilayat Khan stared at her with a look of amazement and disbelief. What an odious encounter this was turning out to be.

After a few moments, she took a deep breath and spoke, 'Yes, Begum Sahiba. I cannot lie. Everyone knows, my past is my past. And it is what it is.'

Vilayat Khan felt a sickening pain shoot through his body, leaving him numb. It was as if someone had vaporised his innermost feelings of love and he had to watch them disappear before his eyes. But this pain, too, was shortlived.

The thing is, the enduring female presence in Vilayat Khan's life was not a human being but a raga: Bhairavi. Everything else fell somewhere between respite and pleasure. It would be a momentary act, perhaps filled with passion, but with a finite quality to it. He couldn't do without women, of course. He played them with the same joy with which he strummed his instrument. But they could never replace his true love. Bhairavi was the one raga he played with heightened ecstasy, and perhaps the raga he played the most times in his life.

Vilayat Khan was raised a Muslim, and was rarely without his prayer beads, but his devotion to the goddess Parvati embodied in raga Bhairavi was purer and more intense than any Hindu priest could have mustered. In his mind, the mythology of Bhairavi and the melodic manifestations of Bhairavi merged into one. Bhairavi was the counterpoint to Bhairav, the raga embodying Shiva.

He once said in an interview: 'I wish I could describe my vision of Bhairav's infinite form and awesome power! I would say the same for Bhairavi. How many different facets of her persona I have envisioned! Oh Allah! By how many different names, and in how many different forms, you manifest yourself to the seeker! It is we who give you different names, according to our limited capacity to understand you. All of them are names in praise of Your Glory. You are masculine; you are also feminine. You are the lover; you are also the beloved. You are the ascetic; you are also the emperor.'

Like so many Muslim musicians, Vilayat Khan's family was originally Hindu. Most of these artistes had converted because their patronage came from the Mughal royalty that ruled over most of India. In this family, fittingly, the reason had been romance. Many years ago, his forefather, a handsome Rajput landowner, fell in love with a woman who was part of a caravan that had travelled to India from Central Asia. He converted to Islam to be with her and that was how the new lineage began. Romance flowed through this family like an underground spring, spurting in the strangest places, sometimes unexpectedly, always in the mode of music.

In 1959, when he was a little over thirty, Vilayat Khan fell in love with and married a dusky Hindu woman called Monisha Hazra whom he met while ballroom dancing at Prince's, Calcutta's swishest club at the Grand Hotel. The daughter of a doctor, she was educated and charming, could play the piano, and connected him to the English-speaking elite world that he aspired to in his constant search for belonging. She slipped with ease into the social life that he had constructed around himself in Bombay, and also learned how to coexist with the relatively simple, uneducated wives of his musician friends, learning from them how to cook classic mutton dishes to please her husband.

By this time, Vilayat Khan had carefully cultivated a dual existence—that of the classical musician, unsurpassable in his talent, and that of a Westernised urban sophisticate who loved social soirees, especially if they were peppered with some debauchery. With equal ease, he mingled with film personalities, classical musicians and businesspersons, embracing the eclectic character of Bombay. He loved his custom-made three-piece suits and equally the kurtas embroidered by his wife. He smoked pipes, delighted in French colognes, played snooker and loved his card games.

In 1965, an article in Bangalore's *Deccan Herald* said:

> Vilayat Khan at 37 has reached a pre-eminence in Indian music world as a Wizard on sitar. He has travelled extensively in the West and his sensitivity to the beauty of music is evenly matched by his taste for good things in life. We may mention in this context, that he has one of the best collections of perfumes from all over the world. As Imrat put it, 'Vilayat Khan has some priceless treasures among them that are more than 250 years old.' He is equally fond of smoking pipes and is reputed to have collections.

He also loved food and believed that the sensory experience of cooking and eating brought aroma into music. Good taste had to be cultivated and it needed to guide all aspects of living. Without appreciating a good biryani, it was impossible to have fine taste in music, he would always tell people.

But one particular obsession of Vilayat's surpassed all others. He loved cars. And he coveted these expensive imported vehicles, not just for their snob value, but also because he admired their sophisticated mechanics. He could tell if there was something amiss in a car's alignment merely by listening to the purr of the engine, such was his relationship with sound.

Soon after Vilayat Khan went to the Festival of Britain in 1951, he acquired a two-seater sports car, which he drove around feeling like the ultimate 'playboy'.

I was going up the elevator in my parents' apartment complex in Bombay one afternoon, when I ran into a dear old family friend, Malti Divecha who lived on the top floor. She asked me what I had been up to and I said that I was on a journey into the life of Vilayat Khan.

She laughed and said, 'Are you serious? Come upstairs to my place, I have something to show you if I can find it.'

In the sixties, Malu and Bhagwan Divecha were part of Bombay's affluent A-listers. They owned several bungalows next to the home of J.R.D. Tata on the tony tree-lined Altamont Road. Malu aunty was bewitchingly beautiful and had raised many envious eyebrows when she modelled a two-piece swimsuit in the fifties. She was a superb hostess, and even her party invitation cards were unique, whether to celebrate her son's birthday or her labrador's litter. I remember being tickled as a child because every time Bhagwan Divecha left the house, he would kiss Malu aunty on her lips. They were modern and harmonious, and Vilayat Khan was a part of their world.

I bypassed my parents' floor and followed Malu aunty upstairs to her flat, into her bedroom, and watched her rummage around in a drawer filled with photographs, old invitation cards and letters. She pulled out an invitation cut in the shape of a car.

She then told me the extraordinary story of Gazzala.

Vilayat Khan had long craved a Mercedes Benz. Finally, in 1964, thanks to the benevolence of his big fan, the king of Afghanistan, that wish came true. Zahir Shah adored Indian classical music and regularly hosted musicians from India. It is said that when an artiste started performing, he would get up from his throne and sit on the floor out of respect for the music. Vilayat Khan was one of his favourites and was invited to Kabul regularly—to play and also teach Prince

Nadir Shah. After a particularly amazing concert at the Kabul Theatre, Zahir Shah asked Vilayat what he could do for him. Vilayat Khan asked for a Mercedes. It was immediately arranged.

By then, Vilayat had enough friends in high places. Someone in the ministry of culture manipulated every rule in the book to get the cobalt blue car into the country despite the strict import regulations of the time. Vilayat Khan made an elaborate plan to drive the car from Kabul, through Pakistan, all the way to Bombay. His brother and a student would accompany him. He was told by the Pakistan authorities that since he didn't have the requisite visas, he could drive through as long as he did not stop, and to ensure this, an army car would accompany him from border to border.

Word got around that Vilayat Khan would be driving through Pakistan. Zulfiqar Ali Bukhari, his old mentor from All India Radio, had moved to Lahore by then, and because of the complications of Partition, had not been able to meet his old musician friends from India. When he learned that his young protégé would be passing through, a few telephone calls were instantly made to get special permission for a brief tea stop. In South Asia, rules are meant to be broken. At four in the morning, Bukhari opened his door to greet Vilayat, and their shouts of joy were so loud that the entire street woke up. Just before sunrise, Khansahib drove across the border into Amritsar, finally reaching Bombay.

Now, he had to show his prize off to the world. He drove it around the city and visited all his friends. Nikhil Ghosh woke up one morning to the door bell ringing and opened the door to see Vilayat Khan in sunglasses, standing in front of his shiny new toy with his little boy Shujaat. He insisted that Nikhil babu and the children get in and go for a spin.

But just driving around was not enough for Vilayat Khan.

This moment had to be celebrated in style. He named the car Gazzala and decided to have an epic party in its honour.

'We were very good friends,' said Malu aunty, her eyes twinkling. 'I knew about all his affairs ... That's another long story, many stories, actually. Anyway, he asked us to throw a party for his Mercedes. He had such a sense of humour. It was also his anniversary. So Monisha and I came up with this!'

She handed me the party invitation. It was in the shape of a car and spoke of twin celebrations—with his new bride Gazzala and his old wife Monisha. I held it awkwardly, respectfully, this rare tangible reminder of a man who was able to transform the smallest event into grand opera.

Soon afterwards, Shiv Vihar was brought down and became Jupiter Apartments, where I spent the first twenty years of my life.

I asked Malu aunty's son Arjun if he remembered the Gazzala party, and he said he did—vividly. He was about ten years old. There was fried pomfret and all varieties of meats and the best imported liquor, and a lot of drunk, happy people. His mother had organised party games and quizzes. Vilayat Khan wore a red-and-green blended silk shirt, and Gazzala was dressed up with a giant nose ring around her impressive bonnet. The party went on till four in the morning.

A few years after the party, Vilayat Khan sent the Divechas a small package. It was a casette recording of him playing a Bengali folk song. It was very rare for him to give his music to anyone. Arjun Divecha, who lives in California, has digitised the music and saved it in his collection of special Bombay heirlooms.

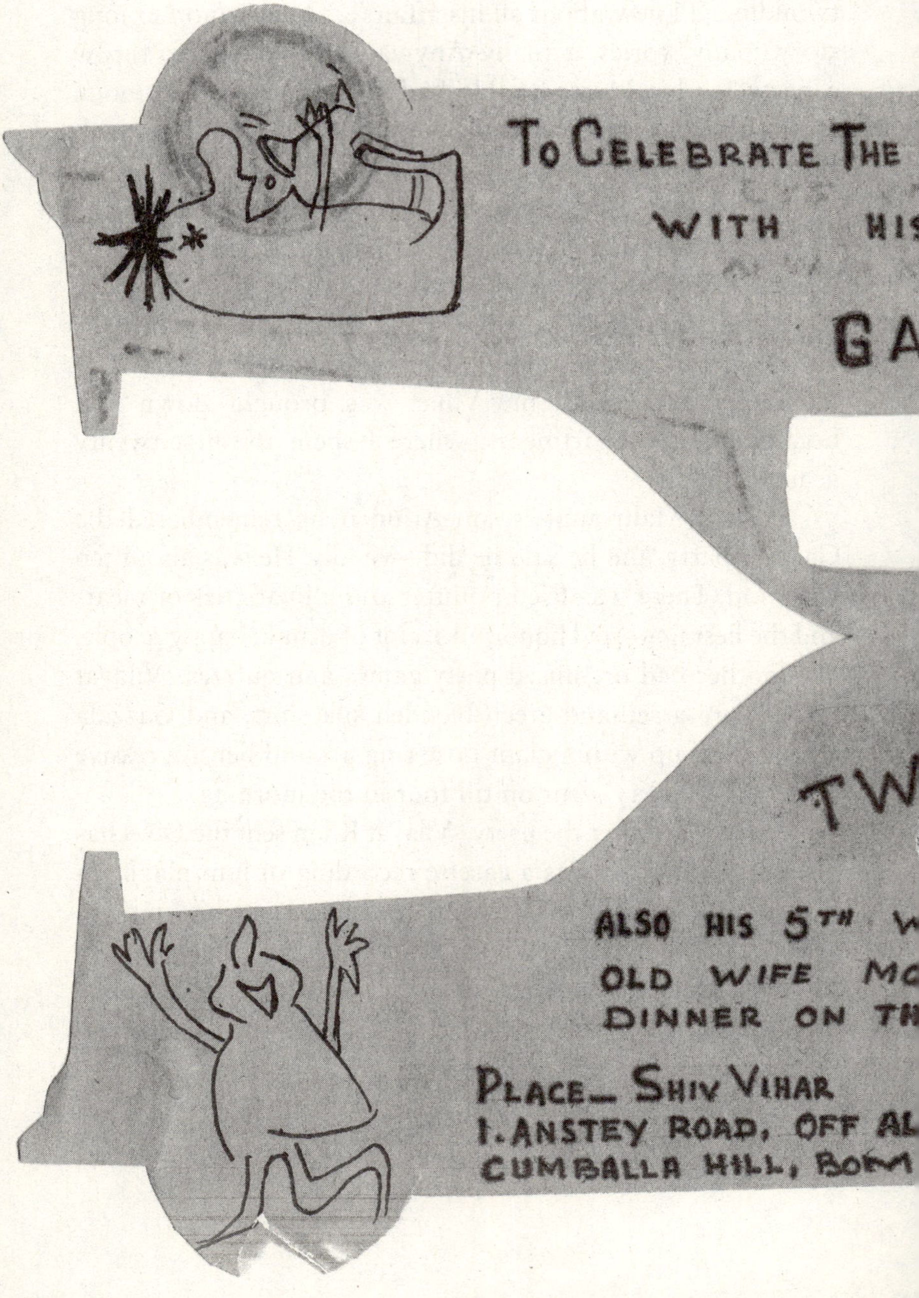
TO CELEBRATE THE
WITH HIS
GA
TW
ALSO HIS 5TH W
OLD WIFE MO
DINNER ON TH
PLACE— SHIV VIHAR
1. ANSTEY ROAD, OFF AL
CUMBALLA HILL, BOM

F VILAYAT KHAN
W BRIDE
LA
CELEBRATION
ANNIVERSARY TO HIS
—YOU ARE INVITED FOR
NOVEMBER 1964.
DRESS—CARELESS.
ROAD
TIME 8-30 PM
TO
R.S.V.P
78821

At the centre of Bombay's historic Kala Ghoda district, surrounded by magnificent Indo-Saracenic architecture, is the Jehangir Art Gallery. It was started by a philanthropic Parsi family in the 1950s. In August 1966, the gallery held a grand exhibition called 'Art and Music through the Ages', choreographed by Vilayat Khan and featuring physical and musical heirlooms from his family.

As visitors walked up the wide steps to the gallery, they were greeeted by vintage golden voices that Vilayat cherished—Jaddan Bai, Abdul Karim Khan, Imdad Khan. Within seconds they were transported to another world, and it was almost as if the instruments on display were playing to them.

One of the most striking pieces was a giant ebony-coloured surbahar 'fashioned out of the wood of an Italian piano belonging to the Tagore family after it got broken', according to a report in the *Evening News of India.* This had been made for Wahid Khan, Vilayat Khan's uncle. Next to it was a toy sitar, one that Vilayat Khan had played as a child. On display was also the gold brocade-and-red velvet choga or gown which was worn by Dada Imdad Khan when he served as court musician in Indore. The green velvet coat of his other grandfather, Bande Hasan Khan, was also exhibited. There were portraits, instruments and other musical artefacts as well.

This was where Shujaat gave his first performance, at the age of six. It is likely that Khansahib decided to organise the exhibition to evoke an aura of charm and grandeur around him, part real and part imagined.

These were times of great accomplishment and great turmoil in Vilayat Khan's life. He was tired. Bombay can have that effect on a celebrity if he was not careful. One day, a friend dropped in at his Nepean Sea Road flat and found him sitting in front of a cabinet in his bedroom, meticulously arranging his collection of miniature glass animals on the shelf.

'Khansahib, what are you doing?'

'Shhh. Don't disturb me, please.'

The visitor watched him obsessively place the little animals in a straight line, each one the exact same distance from the other. When he had finished, he turned around.

'Okay, now I am ready. How are you? Come on in.'

'What were you doing, Khansahib?'

'Well, it is impossible to create perfection in our world, so at least let me manoeuvre it in a small way where I have some control.'

In the mid-sixties, to find peace and some semblance of that perfection, Vilayat Khan left Bombay, with its ceaseless temptations, the surround-sound noise, the pointless partying. This was both the end and the beginning of an important chapter in his life. He kept the flat in Bombay, but retreated with his family to the hills of Shimla, many miles from any concert venue. It was a strange thing to do at the height of his career, but he was never needy for fame.

They moved into a little house on top of Strawberry Hill, and drank their tea under a gigantic tree with yellow flowers the colour of raga Basant.

STRAWBERRY HILL

CHAPTER SEVEN

Life in the Hills

In India, truth is considered overrated. Mythology overwhelms fact. The same story is slightly different in every retelling, like many renditions of a raga. And so it is that there are multiple origin stories for the sitar. One is that it descended from the veena. The story goes that the veena was invented by Shiva, the god of music who lived in solitude in the mountains, where he meditated on his breathing, and through his breath, changed man's destiny. One day, he went into the forest and cut a piece of bamboo. He hollowed out two pumpkins, tied them to the bamboo and strung it with animal guts. When he played this instrument and the deer from the forest heard him, they would say, 'String your instrument with our veins if you like, but please don't stop playing!'

Shimla lies in the lap of the Himalayas, where the hills echo the sound of Shiva's breath and the distant mountains are like ancient shrines. The roar of silence gradually cajoles the restless spirit to merge into its quietude. And inside the silence is music. I went to Shimla, and then beyond, to reconnect with myself and also to find out why Vilayat Khan came here.

In the 1960s, Shimla was a picture-perfect hill station

carved into the slopes of Himachal, which was then part of the Punjab. Because of its altitude, gorgeous weather and the flowers that blossomed in every imaginable colour, it was an antidote to the heat and dust of the plains. When the British discovered it, they made it their summer capital and created a little paradise dotted with cottages and clubs. The rajas from the neighbouring states joined them. It became a summer retreat for the wealthy.

It is hardly surprising that Vilayat Khan was drawn to this place. He first came in 1965 on a summer vacation. That was when he met Padamjit Singh, the former raja of Kapurthala, a music lover and sitar player, who lived in a charming cottage perched on top of a grassy knoll called Strawberry Hill. The raja found a little house called Aira Holme for the Khans to rent for the summer. They came back again the next year and spent even more time there. Vilayat Khan seemed to have found the serenity he was seeking.

It is possible that, around this time, he was a fugitive from his own hedonism. He had done it all and more, and was now ready to surrender, at least partially. The kind of urban decadence that he indulged in could be exhausting, even for one with his energy levels. Shimla would be a respite from it all. He knew, of course, that he was making an anti-career move by retreating to a place where the nearest big concert platform was a seven-hour drive away. Perhaps because he had started so young, and been at it for fifteen years, ennui had begun to set in, and Vilayat Khan now craved tranquillity for long stretches. Then, always, his restless spirit drove him back into the thick of action.

When he went back to Shimla for the second time the following year, Vilayat Khan decided to move there. This time, his friend Padamjit helped him rent Pari Mahal, a sprawling house with many rooms and shrouded by conifer forests, a short distance from the bustling town of Shimla. It once belonged to the raja of Jubbal but had since been taken over by the state government.

Promising the government that he would turn Pari Mahal into a seat of music, Vilayat rented the estate at one rupee a month and started living there with his family. This now included his three children, Shujaat, Yaman and Zila, as well as an extended family that comprised a random assortment of students, a maulvi sahib (when he was not praying or teaching the children the Koran, Khansahib turned him into his card partner), a great cook who could make mutton biryani as well as pancakes, visiting musicians and doting devotees—often young Caucasian women. There was also an enormous chicken coop which housed two black roosters that resembled miniature peacocks. And, of course, that most important member of his family: Gazzala.

After moving in, Vilayat Khan acquired four Himalayan sheepdogs—whimsically named Dinky, Donkey, Jam and Jelly—to guard against encroachers, wild beasts and ghosts, for Pari Mahal was said to have been haunted once. On the nights that the electricity went off, and the stars above shone brighter, and the silence of the surrounding forests loomed inkily, it could very easily have attracted wandering spirits, especially if Khansahib was practising a particular thumri in Bhairavi.

If a blue Mercedes was seen on the slopes of Shimla, the locals knew it belonged to that reclusive sitar player who had come to live in Pari Mahal. A rumour went around that there were only three people whose cars were allowed to enter the pedestrian-only Mall Road in Shimla—the chief minister, the governor and Khansahib.

But the people of Shimla saw his car more than they saw him, for he hardly ventured out. He was content in his musical bubble, inside which he played and taught and drank.

Once in a while, Monisha and he ventured to the colonial-style Green Room to spend an evening, but these moments of intimacy would grow more infrequent as their marriage slowly unravelled.

During this time, Khansahib became close to Padamjit Singh and his family. The two of them spent many hours in each other's homes, playing poker, playing the sitar, having long discussions about particular ragas and why a dha should be shortlived in one, longer in another.

'Do you know how our family became so musical?' Padamjit Singh asked Khansahib one evening, while he was smoking a pipe and sending up a perfectly sculpted plume of smoke. They were seated under the oak tree outside the cottage.

'Because they knew you would eventually become my good friend,' laughed Vilayat Khan.

'When the British disbanded the court of Bahadur Shah Zafar and sent him into exile, there were a number of other casualties. One of the aristocrats, a descendent of Tansen, called Mir Nasir Ahmed, used to sport a long-tailed turban, so the British assumed that he was a senior member of the court and might be a trouble maker. That was when my grandfather, the raja of Kapurthala, assured the governor general that Nasir Ahmed was no rebel but a learned man, a man of music, and that he was willing to take full responsibility for the man's actions. Grandfather took him away to Kapurthala and made Nasir Ahmed his music teacher. His son Mir Rehmat Ali taught my father and me. So that is how it all happened …'

'Yes, yes, in those days, music thrived because of people like your grandfather. They realised the value of music and ensured that everyone had access to it, like food and fuel. They made it a part of the ordinary person's ambient sounds. I remember I was once in Kolhapur for a concert, and I passed a cobbler. As he stitched a slipper, he was humming raga

Malkauns. Can you believe it—the way someone today would hum a Kishore Kumar song! It was his version of Malkauns, of course, but it was Malkauns alright. This is because he had heard it so many times in the court of Shahu Maharaja who loved music and loved his people.'

'Wah janab!'

'It is the zamindars and rajas like all of you who have kept this music alive, definitely not our government. They do nothing. They have no idea how to take care of their artistes. Musicians like my father and Alauddin Khan and Hafiz Ali Khan were nurtured by the raja of Gowripur. That is where I was born. That is where my father really became a great musician, under his patronage.'

'Aah, Gowripur's raja was known for a Japanese palace he built next to his home. He specially brought an architect from Japan to design it. What a man!'

'Now we will have to wait and see who is going to take care of our musicians. I fear the worst for the future. People in Europe are more respectful than people here. I have no regard for the government. Who are they to decide on awards and on radio grading. I have encountered some of the greatest artistes ever, sat at their feet, pressed their legs, heard them sing and play just for me. It made me feel that my birth is worth it and that my life has been successful.'

'Khansahib, those were good days back then,' said Padamjit Singh softly. 'People treated each other differently. The values were different. But we will all have to learn to change with the times.'

'Either that or we will have to move out of this country, Rajaji ...'

Vilayat Khan and Padamjit Singh sat in silence as a whistling thrush started its song, a solo aria set against an obliging orchestra of crickets. It was a sweet, persistent call.

The bird was oblivious of its audience, its music achieving a mysterious unifying goal.

Vilayat Khan was not a hypocrite. He truly believed that artistes existed on a plane several notches higher than most mortals, higher even than the prime minister of the country.

A couple of years earlier, when Jawaharlal Nehru was very ill, one of his doctors had suggested that Vilayat Khan be invited to play for him. Just as Bach's Goldberg Variations were used to heal, Khansahib's music would soothe the prime minister's body and mind and help him sleep restfully. So, every evening, Nehru's secretary would go to the guest house next door and escort the musician to Nehru's bed.

One afternoon, Vilayat Khan was sitting, ready and waiting to be picked up, but when the secretary came, he went to the door, then suddenly stopped, turned around and said, 'Sorry, I am not in the mood to play today.'

'But … but … what do I tell the prime minister?'

'Sorry, I'm not some radio that you can just switch on when you feel like.'

The secretary went back trembling, from one ill-tempered man to another.

'Has Khansahib come?'

'Sir, sir …'

'What is it?'

'Panditji, I'm so sorry, but he said that he was not in the mood.'

Pandit Nehru stared at him. Then he said, 'Please go back and tell him that is fine. When he is in the mood, he can come. I will wait. For I cannot sleep without his music.'

Among their few friends in Shimla was Superintendent of Police Ratiram Varma, a genial, handsome man with the impressive nose of a Rajput warrior. He knew little about music but was drawn to all the artistes who came to live in the region. Varma would regularly entertain J. Swaminathan, the painter, and Vilayat Khan, and listen to their stories. He even respectfully sat through the whole of Vilayat's concert in the glittering ballroom of Shimla's iconic Cecil Hotel.

Ratiram and Vilayat often drank late into the night and ate well, with Khansahib doing most of the drinking and talking, telling stories about his father and grandfather with his usual flair.

'Ratibhai! Let me tell you, the best singer who lived before our time was Zohrabai Agrewali … Uff, what a cheez! What exquisite pain there was in her voice. There has not been one who could sing like that after her.'

Although the police officer was fighting sleep and dreading his crack-of-dawn duty at the governor's bungalow, he adored and admired his guest too much to tell him to stop. Fuelled by a heady cocktail of self-absorption and alcohol, Vilayat Khan then proceeded to sing an entire thumri of Zohrabai which he had learned from her 78 rpm record. He always needed an audience, and when there wasn't one, he would create it.

On warmer days, Khansahib would spend many hours outside on the terrace, surrounded by whoever was staying there at the time, discussing music or playing cards, or bargaining with some cloth merchant who happened to be passing by and had heard that here lived a man with a fetish for exquisite weaves. Vilayat Khan derived great pleasure from buying textiles, and if he struck a good bargain, he would boast about it to everyone.

In those days, Samta Prasad was a regular visitor to Pari Mahal. Prasad was Khansahib's devoted and loyal tabla accompanist who travelled with him all over the world, taking his paan-flecked Banarasi heart with him wherever he went, entirely oblivious to Western etiquette. Vilayat Khan, always so mindful of elegance and manners, loved him and indulged his eccentricities. But there was this one occasion on an airplane, when he told off his friend for behaving as if he was on a village charpoy with cows mooing in the background.

'When we were in Russia, do you know what Samta Prasad did? He swallowed an entire bowl of caviar, thinking it was some form of boondi, and then was so disgusted by the taste that he spat it out right there, at the dining table, on to his plate,' told a gathering that included Samta.

'What rubbish food these people eat, bhaiya,' the tabla player said, digging into an enormous pile of dal and rice and cauliflower cooked exactly to his liking. 'Russia for me was be-rasiya.'

'Samta, do you remember, during that trip, we got a standing ovation, and after I stood up, I kept waiting for you to stand ... But you just sat there with a strange sheepish look. After the curtains went down, you told me the naada of your pajama had come loose!' They both chuckled.

When it started getting cold, the family would leave the hills for Calcutta and go back to the ancestral home in Park Circus, where his brother Imrat Khan and all the children would huddle together in a big room adjoining the courtyard, listening to the stories that Vilayat Khan told, playing and learning music.

During their days together in Calcutta, there would be no differentiation among the children—Vilayat Khan's three and Imrat Khan's five. Vilayat Khan was the elder father, Bade Abba, or just Abba, to everyone. If father and uncle were performing somewhere, the children would fight sleep and try and stay up so that they could listen to stories about the concert later.

They were all uniformly Vilayat Khan's students and the little people of the house; the kitchen was one and the music was one; they would practise together and participate in sticky gulab jamun-eating competitions. Yaman would usually win. Imrat Khan's wife Dulhan was known for her cooking, and the choicest food was always made for a minimum of fifteen people—family, students, and the inevitable hangers-on.

Through the 1950s and most of the sixties, the two brothers were a force to reckon with—masters of two instruments that were independently gorgeous but also complemented each other. When played together, the surbahar creates a penumbra of sound that spreads like a sombre halo around the lighter melodic movements of the sitar. They played together across festivals in India as well as abroad.

There was an implicit understanding in their music, which reflected Imrat's devotion to his elder brother, his teacher, his father figure. Through his childhood, he had followed 'bade bhaiya' around like a happy puppy. As he grew older, he was happy to shadow and echo him, and had no desire to compete. Even when they sat together on stage for a duet, he used to sit just a little behind Vilayat in quiet deference.

There was no question about who was the star among the two. Sometimes, when they were playing together, it seemed as if Vilayat Khan became so absorbed in his own music that he had forgotten his brother was sitting next to him.

A newspaper review of their duet at Delhi's Shankarlal Festival in 1964 gave a hint of this:

> The best item on the bill was yet another jugalbandi, this time with Vilayat Khan on sitar and Imrat Khan on surbahar. Imrat Khan, whenever he got an opportunity, played consistently good and handled the notes with great tenderness.

Imrat Khan was in his late twenties at this time, and coming into his own as an independent artiste, but the equation between them remained as before. It is likely that Basheeran Begum kept her sons together, seeing their collective potential. The winter months in the Park Circus house was where a lot of wrinkles got ironed out.

When the cold receded, well before Megh and Malhar darkened the skies, Vilayat Khan would be back in the hills, now covered with purple irises and crimson roses the size of tennis balls.

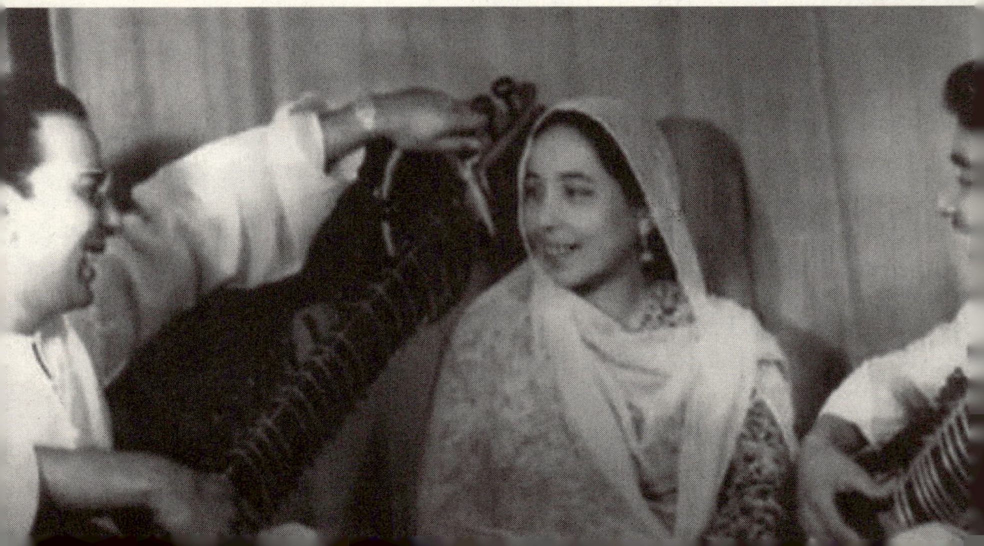

Shujaat was enrolled in the Jesuit-run Bishop Cotton School in Shimla. Studies and sports during the day; sitar at night, or early in the morning, if his father was around and forced him to wake up. The boy had already been called a little master after his debut concert at the Jehangir Art Gallery in Bombay. His musical tutelage was all planned. He had been given a toy sitar as a baby and used to play with it. Then it was taken away, and when he clamoured for it, his parents said they would give him the real thing, but he had to play it properly.

While his father's luminous presence and music was always around him, Shujaat did not see him all that much. Vilayat Khan would be out of the country for long stretches. Even when he was home, there were always others in his orbit, and Shujaat had to find his place within it, fight for his father's attention, which was diverted by acolytes, drinking and the increasingly depressing fights with Monisha. He felt as if he was falling in slow motion into the abyss that was growing between his parents. The casual cruelty they inflicted on each other left little room for love, and even less time for him or his two little sisters. He found solace in basketball and cricket, in the sitar and in the compassion of the family's loyal helper, Ratna.

And yet, as always happens within the darkness of family life, there were startling moments of light—like on that cold and rainy evening when the temperature suddenly dipped.

Vilayat Khan had just returned from a trip to England, and had brought back Cadbury's Bournville drinking chocolate. He was very excited to introduce his son to this delicious drink. He stirred up two steaming mugs in the kitchen and brought them out to the porch along with two quilts. He wrapped one around the boy and the other around himself, and they sat there, in silence, holding their mugs. It was freezing. In front of them was the dark silouhette of pine trees fringing the hills.

'Beta, you know this feeling you are experiencing right now? This whole picture of us sitting here—the inky trees all around us, the sky a lighter shade of black, the cold you are feeling outside, the warmth and comfort you feel inside, this utterly gorgeous moment ... You have to learn to transcribe all these feelings and this beauty into your music. It is not about the notes but what goes on behind those notes. This is why a musician's son will always be different from one who comes to learn music. These are things that cannot be taught, they have to be experienced. Every experience must translate into your music. That's all there is for you to remember. You, my firstborn, will play like a king one day.'

Shujaat cuddled closer to his father and his eyes brimmed over. He was overwhelmed with respect and love. He sensed that rare moment of connection, something he would crave for the rest of his life for it came to him only sporadically. But when it did, it was steeped in intensity.

When Shujaat was a little older, he and his father were driving from Bombay to Shimla. They sped through the night, and just as dawn was breaking, entered the state of Rajasthan. Vilayat stopped and got out to have a cigarette. Then he said, in a soft undertone, as if not to disturb the rising sun, 'Shujaat, beta, look!'

An orange-and-gold sun was emerging in the distance and they could hear soft singing. A group of village women in bright colours were walking towards the well to wash and bathe and fill their vessels.

'If we stand here for another half an hour or so, you'll see them come back and they will be swaying differently. They will look different. The way they look when they are coming back, that is the picture you have to translate into your music ... There is a deep relationship between colour and sound and beauty. They feed one another, they create harmony.'

Many years later, the warm afterglow of these moments with his father would float into Shujaat's dreams—and into his music.

Early in 1968, Vilayat Khan received a message from the Government of India telling him that he had been awarded the Padma Shri. Instead of feeling pleased, Khansahib turned to those sitting around him and launched into a diatribe against the government. It was a longstanding grouse. He believed that no bureaucrat had the authority to decide who was musically better or deserving. He had stopped performing on All India Radio because he was fiercely opposed to the idea of artistes being graded and accordingly awarded time slots and fees. He sent a message back refusing the award. He was then offered the next level award, the Padma Bhushan, which he also turned down. It reinforced his belief that the government award system for artistes was arbitrary and insulting. He took every opportunity to vocalise his views.

He once told a newspaper reporter, 'They call me moody and whimsical because I have such strong views. I am only asking one question. On what basis do they decide which musician deserves an award? Is it our age? Is it our good looks? Is it where I live? No one has been able to answer that question, so I am going to opt out.'

Around the same time, an unlikely visitor showed up at Pari Mahal. He was an income tax officer who had decided to find out why this famous musician, whose stature was only growing, had never filed his tax returns.

Khansahib invited him to have lunch, and they ate a lavish meal of chicken curry, mutton korma, three different vegetables, and the most delicious creamy kheer for dessert.

'Khansahib, you are living in such a big house, surrounded by so many people, eating so well. Where is all this income of yours coming from and what about tax?'

Vilayat Khan looked at him, widened his eyes and raised his eyebrows, feigning complete surprise, like a child pretending that no one else could see his hand in the cookie jar.

'Income tax? But what income are you referring to, sahib? I am a mere musician. You know how badly we are treated. Where is the question of money? Even this house we are living in is haunted. But we have nowhere else to go. Let me play for you, though.'

He did. A happy little piece in raga Bihari which he had composed for Satyajit Ray's *Jalsaghar* some years earlier. The income tax official sat quietly. When the music was over, he left with a quick goodbye, never to return.

I found my way to Pari Mahal, twisting and turning through the traffic-choked roads of present-day Shimla. Honey Singh was blaring from a van parked outside the building. Pari Mahal now houses the Himachal Pradesh State Health and Family Welfare Training Centre, where government doctors are taught how to administer the polio vaccine. The building was painted a nauseous pink, as if someone was intent on killing beauty. Most of the windows were boarded up.

I went inside, foolishly expecting to stumble into a museum of music, or some remnant of the glory days—a broken tabla lying discarded in a corner, perhaps once played by Lohmi or Mansha Khan, the local tabaliyas who used to accompany Khansahib when he practised. But the rooms inside looked like any other soulless government office with glass-topped desks, bulky desktop computers and ugly upholstery. I asked an official seated behind a desk whether she might know anything about the time Vilayat Khan lived here. She stared at me blankly.

An old retainer walked past her room just then and she called out to him, 'Arre, Ayodhyaji, did some sarod or sitar player once live here?'

He said, 'Yes, madam. His name was Vilayat Khan. That was some forty-fifty years ago, even before my time. There is a plaque outside the gate which has some information about this.'

At least someone remembered him, someone other than the misty pine trees, which were around long before he came and endured long after he left. I knew why he had come here, but why did he leave?

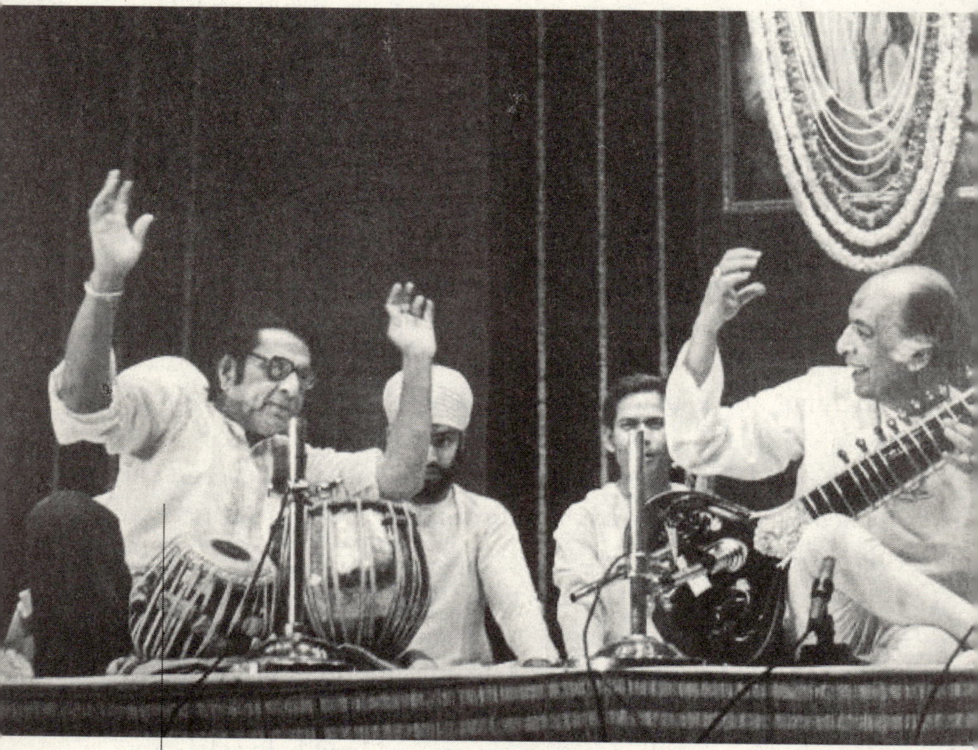

Samta Prasad

CHAPTER EIGHT

The Foreign Circuit

The Western world was first introduced to Indian music sometime in the early 1900s when a musician and sufi scholar called Hazrat Inayat Khan travelled to America and introduced audiences to a sound they had never heard before. He played the veena and sang, but did not gather much of an audience. Gradually, he stopped playing what he called 'struck music' and turned his attention to exploring the mysticism of sound, how 'unstruck music' flows in and around us. He integrated sufi thought and music into a series of beautiful essays.

In his book, *The Mysticism of Music, Sound and Word*, he wrote:

> I gave up music because I had received from it all that I had to receive … I arrived at a stage where I touched the music of the spheres. Then every soul became for me a musical note, and all life became music … Now, if I do anything, it is to tune souls instead of instruments; to harmonize people instead of notes. If there is anything in my philosophy, it is the law of harmony: that one must put oneself in harmony with oneself and with others. I have found in every word a certain musical value, a melody in every thought, harmony in every feeling; and I have tried to interpret the same thing,

> with clear and simple words, to those who used to listen to my music ...

In the early 1950s, similar ideas about the potency of Indian music and its capacity to create harmonies within and among people travelled into the mind of the great master violinist Yehudi Menuhin. Long before the term 'world music' was coined, Menuhin became its biggest missionary. Although he was raised in America, he always turned to other cultures for inspiration. He wrote about his fascination with India in his memoir, *Unfinished Journey*:

> Having grown up in competitive America where survival was by will power and pesticides, I could not find other than marvelous a world which drew its strength from the encouragement of so much life and the destruction of so little ... To belong to such continuity relieves the individual, I think, of much of the burden of uniqueness. Life and death are not all and nothing, but stages in a process, episodes on an infinite river to which one trusts oneself and all other phenomena. So, it is that Indian music reflects Indian life, having no predetermined beginning or end but flowing without interruption through the fingers of the composer–performer; the tuning of the instrument merges imperceptibly with the elaboration of the melody, which may spin itself out for two, three or more unbroken hours.
>
> Melodically and rhythmically, Indian music long ago achieved a complex sophistication which only in the twentieth century, with the work of Bartok and Stravinksy, has Western music begun to adumbrate ... What Indian music has not, and Western music richly has, is, of course, harmony. This is not fortuitous. Just because the Indian would unite himself with the infinite rather than with his neighbour, so his music assists the venture.

In 1952, Menuhin was invited by the Indian government to give a series of performances in Bombay, Delhi, Calcutta, Bangalore and Madras. He socialised with the Nehrus, befriended Ravi Shankar, learned under the yoga guru B.K.S. Iyengar, and was smitten by Indian philosophy. Menuhin decided that he would bring the sound of Indian strings to the global stage.

Clearly, the West was ready. The international cross-currents were flowing more strongly than ever. Exhausted with its arrogance and rapacious errors, people in the West had started turning to India as a space of healing. It was the time of Karma Cola. Things Indian became fashionable. Along with godmen, hashish and yoga, people were touched by Indian music. Besides Menuhin, the Beatles, John Cage and Philip Glass had been seeking sounds outside their known notes and scales. Bob Dylan discovered the Bengali singing mystics; John Coltrane explored half-tone riffs in his jazz music. People were seeking answers in those undecipherable microtones and unseen notes that can never quite be transcribed, nor fully owned, realising perhaps that life's rational, perceived notes have limitations.

In 1955, an inspired Menuhin arranged a festival at the New York's Museum of Modern Art, called 'The Living Arts of India' and featuring musicians and dancers from north India. Menuhin had initially invited Ravi Shankar, but his personal life was going through a rough patch so he coaxed his friend and brother-in-law Ali Akbar Khan to go in his place. Khan obliged, though somewhat reluctantly.

Ali Akbar Khan was accompanied by Chatur Lal on the tabla. There was visible excitement about this amazing new sound that people had not heard before.

The eminent classical music critic Winthrop Sargeant reviewed the concert in *The New Yorker*: 'One is struck by [the music's] great differences from our own; one conjures up all sorts of tropical and picturesque associations ... I found their music endlessly fascinating from a technical point of view and curiously hypnotic in its emotional effect.'

Until then, Indian classical music had been recorded only for the Indian market. It was in 1955 that a Western record label took a chance and published its first album of Indian music. Angel Records set up a recording studio inside the Museum of Modern Art guest house where the artistes were staying. Ali Akbar Khan played two marvellous pieces, accompanied by Chatur Lal. The music was preceded by a thoughtful and considered commentary by Menuhin. The album, which was called *Music of India*, was republished many years later, titled *Then and Now*, and got nominated for a Grammy.

Indian musicians began getting invited to Europe and America to perform, to feature on television and radio, and to teach. Around this time, Menuhin fell in love with and married an English dancer and moved to London. It is here that he spent most of the rest of his life, continuing to promote Indian classical music and artistes whenever he could. He started bringing Indian artistes to Britain, especially to the Edinburgh Festival.

In 1958, the following item appeared in *The Times of India*'s 'Social Whirl' column, written by someone who went by the pen name Pollux:

> On June 14, 1958, the celebrated violinist Yehudi Menhuin entertained two Indian musicians to a cocktail party in London—Vilayat Khan and his tabla accompanist Nikhil Ghosh. The gathering included internationally famous musicians, composers, conductors and critics.

Vilayat Khan had started travelling to England and Europe in the early fifties. In the summer of 1958, he did an extended tour, which included a big performance at the Royal Festival Hall in London. According to a local newspaper report, the hall was packed, and in attendance were the acting Indian High Commissioner Azim Hussain 'and several distinguished people including ambassadors, members of parliament, musicians and literary men'. He spent the next few weeks performing across London, as well as in places like Devon, Birmingham and Oxford, to enthusiastic audiences.

Vilayat Khan clearly loved the flavour of the West because it was so different from the politics of music in India. During a radio interview with BBC in London, sometime in the sixties, he was asked to compare the audiences in India with those in Britain and he said, 'Well, you know, the problem in India is that there is so much ooh-ing and aah-ing; I prefer the quietness of audiences here.'

This was followed by a series of regular trips across Europe for concerts, mostly with Imrat Khan. In 1959, Vilayat was awarded a silver medal at the First Moscow International Film Festival for his music direction in Satyajit Ray's *Jalsaghar.*

The appreciation for Indian classical music only kept growing across Europe and America. A few years later, Ali Akbar Khan got invited to teach at McGill University in Montreal, Canada. But the magical musical bridge between East and West came in the form of Ravi Shankar who, at a very young age, had become a veteran world traveller with his brother Uday Shankar's dance company, and was extremely comfortable catering to non-Indian audiences.

In the summer of 1967, a ridiculously handsome young Ravi Shankar and Alla Rakha played together on an open-air stage at the Monterey rock festival in California, creating an atmosphere that would go down in history. The audience included Janis Joplin and Jimi Hendrix. A YouTube video captures not just Ravi Shankar's playing, but also the expressions of people in the audience who—even if partly altered by mood-enhancing drugs—look stunned, mesmerised, blown, as if they had been transported to another planet and were experiencing something new and amazing.

By this time, Ravi Shankar had already started collaborating with the Beatles, and found an obsessed student in George Harrison who came to India to learn from him. The quaint plaintive sitar playing in 'Norwegian Wood' and *Sergeant Pepper's Lonely Hearts Club Band* had hit the radio waves across the world. Suddenly, Indian music became the new new thing.

Responding to this growing demand, Ali Akbar Khan decided to start a college of Indian music in northern California. When he announced this decision to his friend, the Buddhist practitioner Alan Watts, the latter called up a wealthy associate, who arrived that very evening with a cheque for 20,000 dollars to get the college started. The college, which was set up in 1967, became another milestone, with Indian musicians coming regularly from India to teach there. That same year, Ravi Shankar, Alla Rakha and Yehudi Menuhin collaborated on an album called *West Meets East*, which went viral across the world.

In 1971, George Harrison persuaded Ravi Shankar to use music as a medium for political expression—the iconic Concert for Bangladesh. They all played in New York's Madison Square Gardens, along with Bob Dylan, George Harrison and Eric Clapton, which suddenly put the problems of this tiny newborn country on the global map. The audience was so unaccustomed to the sound of Indian music that they started clapping right after the musicians had tuned their instruments!

In his book, *The Dawn of Indian Music in the West*, Peter Lavezzoli wrote about the Concert for Bangladesh which he attended as a young boy, 'It is difficult to express the sense of wonder I experienced hearing this music for the first time, but I knew it was something I would want to hear again.' He was fascinated with all the new instruments and said about the tabla, 'With the laces running down the side and the big black spot on top, they looked more like cupcakes than drums.'

For Ravi Shankar, the excitement of collaboration and creativity overrode any fear of criticism from the puritanical pedagogues back home. Because of his openness and enthusiasm, he was embraced by musicians hungry for new and expansive sounds. As George Harrison wrote in the introduction to Ravi Shankar's book, *Raga Mala*: 'For him to go and study for seven years, eighteen hours a day, and become master of an instrument which was obscure in most of the world, and for which nobody was particularly craving outside India, and then spend the rest of his life trying to hip everybody to it—what a thing to do!'

Ravi Shankar's early international exposure and his felicity with English empowered him to tailor his recitals for Western audiences, shortening the ragas, explaining things like why a particular raga is played at sunset or during summer. He said in an interview:

> I never compromised on style; I never compromised in giving them anything un-Indian in a bid to please them. All I did was to reduce the duration. Instead of one or two ragas in two or three hours, I played maybe four ragas within two hours, with an intermission and explained to them the ascending and descending of a particular raga, what mood it creates, whether it belongs to the morning or evening, whether it belongs to spring or the rainy season and so forth. The result could be seen immediately. They could understand and accept our music.

One of the first reviews of his music was written by John Rockwell, who eventually became a respected music critic with *The New York Times*, and known for promoting Indian classical music. He was then a young reporter in Berkeley and wrote in the *Oakland Tribune*:

> Before a half-full house of flower children, amidst clouds of incense and the vast ugly spaces of the Berkeley Community

> Theater, with seraphic Western ladies in saris distributing announcements for a meditation session of the International Society for Krishna Consciousness, with bullnecked gentlemen hawking dollar programs, Ravi Shankar, sitar, and Alla Rakha, tabla, with Kamala Chakravarty, tamboura, appeared Saturday night in recital.
>
> Through it all, Ravi Shankar remains one of the supremely great musicians of our time. Of course he has written movie scores—good ones—but when he plays in the classical style he is both faithful and creative. Those who put him down simply don't know what they are talking about.

Vilayat Khan was constantly confronted with the presence—even in absence—of Ravi Shankar, especially while performing in England and Europe. For example, a report in a local Devon newspaper where he played in 1968 stated:

> The only sitar player to hold a candle to Beatle George Harrison's friend Ravi Shankar appears at the Lobster Pot, Instow, near Bedford on Friday. He is Ustad Vilayat Khan, who appears with his brother in the first concert recital of Indian music to be held in North Devon.

But Vilayat Khan's narrative on this subject was clear. Whenever he was interviewed on the subject of Ravi Shankar, he would unequivocally place himself in a different slot from him. A London newspaper, *The Evening News*, reported Vilayat Khan's views on Ravi Shankar:

> At the mention of Ravi Shankar, the most famous sitarist in the West due mainly to his tutoring of George Harrison, Vilayat Khan was silent a moment, staring out of the window. 'Shankar started very late ...' he said. 'But in 1946, we all thought him a genius. But now ... it is not the same. Perhaps he could come back if he stops the commercialisation.'

Vilayat Khan was clearly making his own mark. In 1968, the Indian government presented him, along with other illustrious Indians, to the queen of England at Buckingham Palace's annual garden party. Vilayat Khan wore his best Savile Row suit for the occasion.

The following year, Westminster Abbey hosted its first ever concert of Indian classical music and invited Vilayat Khan to perform. Just before the concert, the organisers spoke in hushed whispers to the musicians. 'You will be sitting on a 900-year-old carpet. So do be a bit careful.'

Vilayat Khan winked at his old friend Sankha Chatterjee, who was accompanying him on the tabla. When they started playing, they were astounded at the tremendous echo within the Abbey. The musicians had never been in an accoustic environment like this before. Vilayat Khan leaned over to his accompanist and said, 'Hey Sankha, play a bit more softly. Let us try and incorporate the reverberation and make it a part of the music.'

'Yes, dada.'

Destiny travels in strange ways, like a moonbeam which has touched an individual and then touches another in a completely different part of the world, somehow intertwining their lives. In 1969, two young college-going New Yorkers—Lyle Wachovsky, a senior majoring in medieval history, and Misha Schreiber, a freshman training in classical cello—attended a class on the basics of Indian classical music at the City College of New York. It was taught by Ravi Shankar. Alla Rakha, who was with him, was teaching a course in the basics of tabla and Misha became his student.

Lyle and Misha scarcely knew it at the time, but what

took place in their heads and hearts at that time would play a significant role in bringing Vilayat Khan to America some twenty years later.

Indeed, many musical seeds were being sown at this time. On the other side of the world, in London, a young artist called Robert Browning, who used to listen to BBC radio music while painting, suddenly stopped mid-brush stroke. He had never heard this sound before. It was an incredibly plaintive string instrument with a deep bass tone. He waited till the end and heard the name of the artiste: Imrat Khan from India. It stayed with him and became an important marker in a journey that would eventually make Browning one of the pioneers of world music in New York.

These were all people looking for something new. One New York jazz musician says the scent of patchouli still aroused in him a memory of listening to the radio in his parents' house, and hearing the strange new sound of strings in the song 'Norwegian Wood'. While for many this was a happy blurry passing phase, people like Misha and Lyle and Robert stayed on.

It was during Vilayat Khan's foreign circuit that the first signs of trouble between him and his brother started revealing themselves. While Vilayat Khan had already been performing abroad, a series of breathtaking duets in Britain in the early 1960s launched Imrat Khan's career there.

Imrat Khan was always one step behind his elder brother, and for the longest time it worked for both. In a note published in a brochure for the Edinburgh Festival where they were both playing, the eminent cultural critic V.K. Narayana Menon wrote:

> Imrat Khan, like his brother, is the inheritor of a great tradition. This, coupled with the training he has been receiving from his brother, is responsible for the place he occupies in the field of music today. Judging by what he has already achieved, it is to be hoped that he will soon follow in the footsteps of his brilliant brother.

As Imrat Khan grew into a man and an artiste, he began to sense that his brother was deliberately curbing his growth as a musician in his own right. He caught on that it was not merely artistic immersiveness, but something faintly disturbing, which was so imperceptible that only he could tell, just the way a wife can just sense when her husband is lying. At a duet concert at the Royal Festival Hall in Britain in the early 1960s, while they played together, Imrat Khan noticed that the applause for him was making his brother irritable, and with each successive round of clapping, Vilayat Khan saw to it that Imrat played even less.

Imrat Khan started feeling the desperate need to break away—even if for a short while—and the opportunity came to him in the form of a long teaching assignment in Dartington College of Arts in Devon.

The cracks began showing in small ways at first and, later, in a series of fights which became public humiliations. Musicians may be magicians when it comes to their art, but when the lights go down, they become human and are besieged by the same mortal imperatives that fragment so many business families—ego, greed and power dynamics.

At the heart of it was the narcissism of an elder brother who had grown used to having his way with most people, and a younger brother who knew he did not have the other's rock star personality but was finding his own space. He no longer wanted to be controlled.

A lion and a tiger cannot be in the same room.

It was while they were on a foreign tour in the early sixties that the troubles came to the fore. The rifts were fuelled by people around them, knowingly or unwittingly—music agents and promoters, possessive and protective students, accompanists, relatives—and by that unstoppable force called destiny. Imrat Khan had been invited to perform at Queen Elizabeth Hall. The concert was sold out. This was the beginning of his brother's independent career in Europe, and it may have irked Vilayat Khan.

Family members suggest that Basheeran Begum also slyly played her sons against each other in an attempt to retain control over both as well as over the growing family wealth. She encouraged Imrat Khan to do things behind his brother's back. Concert organisers would be fed incorrect information about Vilayat Khan's availability and there were growing trust issues.

And yet, despite everything, in 1967, the two of them recorded an album together for His Master's Voice in Mumbai which became one of the most beautiful instrumental duets of all time. The record was titled *A Night at the Taj*. The raga was Chandni Kedar and they were accompanied on the tabla by Nizamuddin Khan.

The eternally romantic Vilayat Khan had visualised the entire piece, start to finish. He created a musical story of Shah Jahan and Mumtaz Mahal whose souls had been given permission to take human form for one full moon night and come down to earth and dance around the Taj Mahal. For the first time, Mumtaz saw what her beloved had built for her. They danced into the night, the sitar personifying the beauteous queen and the more bass surbahar playing the king, echoing her in contrapuntal movements of perfect harmony and utter adoration. In the end, the tempo slows down and there is a short sombre moment when the two souls realise that they are not human, their time is up, and they have to part ways and go back where they came from.

The musician G.N. Joshi, who worked for HMV, wrote the following note on the record sleeve:

> For the first time in the history of Indian classical disc-music, an attempt has been made to present through the media of instrumental performance, an artiste's conception of a universally known theme. It was woven around an imaginary incident involving that immortal pair of lovers, Shahjehan, the creator of Taj Mahal, and his wife Mumtaz. Their souls, restless in heaven, are yearning for an opportunity to revisit their temple of love...
>
> Here goes, as we begin to play the opening side, the story in its chronological sequence as visualised by the artistes. The angels escort the souls of Mumtaz and Shahjehan from the heavens down to earth and they descend musically on the vast gardens of the Taj.
>
> The alaps that follow take us with the pair who are sauntering in the garden—full of fragrant bloom—hand in hand—now pausing to appreciate the colourful beauty of roses, moving on again, looking from different angles, spots of beauty which they alone knew...
>
> And now, warmed up in love, they enter into their past life—the period before their wedding. The longing to meet, the fond remembrances of clandestine meetings, the hundred and one innocent pranks played by them on each other in mischief. A desire awakens in Shahjehan to consummate his love...
>
> The curtain rises on the second side with a slow rhythmic movement portraying their life together—depicting Love, Passion, Pathos, Joy—all the various facets of life—the different ways in which they enjoy—discarding all the norms of convention and throwing away all barriers of social customs ...
>
> And alas! And all of a sudden there is a bolt from the blue—a complete break in all this heavenly bliss. Mumtaz's heart full of love beats no more. For Shahjehan, there exists no life—no power—no desire—everything is meaningless

except the haunting memories of the one he loved—of the one he possessed, and of the one he had enjoyed.

The angels reappear because the period of parole is over. The couple is told that their time is up and they must return forthwith to their heavenly abode. Mumtaz hesitates—then boldly takes the lead with her lover. They are sad and return reluctantly, leaving behind a tear in stone—that is to be the glory of their immortal love and one of the wonders of the world.

A year later, this ode to love created by the two of them gave way to loathing. Vilayat Khan had been picked as one of four accomplished Indians whom the government of India decided to present to the queen of England at a tea party at Buckingham Palace. The Indian High Commissioner, S.S. Dhawan, came to pick the two brothers up from their house in Golders Green. Vilayat Khan was visibly edgy and they drove along in silence. Dhawan, who was sitting in front, suddenly turned around and addressed Imrat Khan.

'We will not be able to take you to Buckingham Palace unless you wear a tie.'

'I don't wear ties,' Imrat Khan replied.

The driver of the car politely intervened and said he would be happy to loan the one he was wearing.

'How can I wear a tie? I am wearing a bush shirt.' Imrat Khan was getting angry at this sartorial diktat and looked at his brother to intervene on his behalf. Vilayat Khan had been silent all through the conversation, but then spoke.

'If you are not going to take heed, Imrat, then please do not come,' said Vilayat.

Imrat Khan stared at his older brother in disbelief. For years, he had been overlooking slights and hurts. It's the mind's oldest form of defence and hope. This was the final blow.

Vilayat Khan looked in the other direction at the houses they were driving past. He then asked the driver to stop the car. He reached out across his younger brother and opened the door. Without saying a word, Imrat Khan got out, eyes smarting with humiliation. He stood on the kerb at Marble Arch for a few minutes, not fully fathoming what had just happened. He realised, as the car sped away, that he didn't have a penny in his pocket and that he would have to walk back almost two hours to Golders Green. He decided during that walk that he would no longer depend on his brother for anything—not for money, not for love, not for music.

After that, their relationship went downhill.

At some point, in an attempt to bandage the relationship, the family arranged betrothals between the children. Vilayat Khan's son Shujaat and daughter Yaman were engaged to Imrat Khan's daughter Sabiha and son Nishat Khan, respectively. Not surprisingly, the engagements broke up. The young people were mismatched and already too independent, and eventually each of them picked their own partners.

The last straw on the camel's back was Imrat Khan's collusion with his sisters and mother to take over their share of the Park Circus house so that it became entirely his. His version of the story is that he was handling the cost of its maintenance and repair and his brother did not contribute towards its upkeep even though he kept coming back to it. Vilayat Khan felt no need to present a justification. By the mid-1970s, the separation was formalised, and that childhood home was no longer available for his use. Vilayat Khan was livid. It is something he never quite got over, and always held against his brother and sisters.

When Vilayat Khan trusted someone, that person could do no wrong, but the moment the relationship got corroded, he never looked back.

By this time, Imrat Khan's four sons were establishing themselves on the music circuit across India and abroad, and he had to support them. Nishat Khan was a highly accomplished sitar player, Irshad played the surbahar, Shafatullah the tabla, Wajahat the sarod. They played the music of Enayat Khan and Imdad Khan.

For the moon to shine, the sun has to be extinguished. By the mid-seventies, Imrat Khan had realised that he would have nothing more to do with his famous and flamboyant brother who, he said wryly, 'liked to keep the company of maharajas and partake in that kind of lavish lifestyle'.

Imrat Khan had started spending more and more time abroad—in Berlin, in London—and finally got a teaching assignment in the US, at Washington University in St Louis, Missourie. This is where he met Belinda, his student who would become his wife. Their young son Azmat Ali is being trained in sitar and surbahar, and is a delightful mixture of two worlds.

But even if he kept his distance, Imrat Khan encouraged his sons to go to his brother's concerts and later keenly listened to their reports, asking minute details about his music or what he was wearing. Nishat remained close to his uncle and availed of every opportunity to learn from him.

Nishat remembers that, sometime in the seventies, Vilayat Khan was in the Park Circus house, practising raga Hameer. Nishat and a few others were sitting around him, enveloped in a bubble of sound that was both magnificent and peaceful. Suddenly Vilayat Khan did something so subtle and so elegant with the two madhyam notes that Nishat, who was sitting in front of him, said 'Subhanallah!' softly and immediately lowered his eyes. For, with the elders in the music world, there was an unwritten protocol even in the expression of appreciation.

St Louis is an underwhelming city in the middle of America, known for its high crime rate and not much else. But there are worlds within worlds, even when you cannot see them.

I had been filled with trepidation at the thought of meeting Imrat Khan, because I was writing about his brother who had scorned him in public, not once but many times. The last time was when, at a grand public gathering in Delhi, Imrat Khan had placed a shawl at Vilayat Khan's feet. His elder brother just turned the other way.

But when I walked in, an adorable old man wearing a cap and flannel pajamas greeted me with warmth. I touched his feet and he said, '*Khush raho*. Stay blessed. I am so glad you have come. I am glad you are writing about our family.'

His home was filled with photographs of his father, his mother, his sons and even his brother. At the centre was a picture of Vilayat Khan on the sitar and Imrat Khan on the surbahar with the portraits of their father and grandfather behind them. It was a blow up of the album cover of *A Night at the Taj*.

Over the next two days, I discovered that he had just survived an almost-fatal stroke and was now scarcely able to play the surbahar. He drifted in and out of many memories—their time in Bhujwari Mohalla on Zakaria Street in Bombay when he used to press his brother's back as well as iron his clothes; their days in the Park Circus house in Calcutta; the time he bought his first white Mercedes in Cologne and how his brother felt jealous. He spoke about their mother, who had been the strongest person in their lives while they were growing up, bereft of a proper home or father or teacher. How she ensured that he got proper training befitting the son of Enayat Khan from wherever she could extract it, using all the resources she had.

In the midst of the conversations, he would keep reaching out to 'Billi' which is what he called his wife, and she called him 'Ustadji', at least in public. His eyes lit up the moment his son, Azmat, a handsome little fellow, came back from school and gave him a hug. '*Mera baccha* ... How was your day?'

'Pure Vilayat Khan taleem came only to me, not even to his sons. As long as we were together, he had such control over me that I used to think that even if he gave me poison I would drink it. For many years, I was proud to be his chamcha. I loved him so much that I accepted my position as that. I took pride in it …' He started weeping. 'I loved him more than anything in the world.'

I froze with remorse at having scratched open an old scab and unleashed so much pain. Belinda gestured to me not to worry, to let him keep talking.

'I cannot say anything more. I knew how great he was. I only want to remember him as that. I cannot tell you all the things he did to me. I don't want to. I became so famous in Europe that whatever he wanted to do, I was already doing.'

Memory is like a construction site, where the scaffolding may be factual but much of the material is selective nostalgia. What is completely and absolutely real is the music—which is what I found out on my last night there. My flight was cancelled due to bad weather and I was back in the house. But I didn't want to make Khansahib talk anymore, so we listened to *A Night at the Taj*. We were silent, except when Imrat Khan would tell a bit of the story, how the angels came, how these two lovers were playing, and then the sadness. He pointed out how he was only echoing his brother softly, shadowing him at a lower volume, never overplaying.

'Listen to his amazing sitar. Subhanallah! This is a taan of our fathers and forefathers … aaaah … what beauty … Only bhaiya can play like this. If anyone else is playing this kind of music, this right-hand technique, they are merely imitating him.'

His eyes filled up again. Hate is the other side of love. For those few moments in the full moon night under the Taj Mahal, in suburban St Louis, there was only love and beauty.

The music ended with a sense of deep melancholy as the angels came down to gently escort the two up. Their time as lovers was over. Perhaps I was imagining it, but we had entered the silence of clemency.

'I never want to be Ustad Vilayat Khan. Neither his music, nor his personality,' he said softly. No one spoke after that, and I left early the next morning.

Perhaps if there had been no Vilayat Khan, Imrat Khan would have been a great star. Then again, in music, or in any art, can there really be a number one? Is that not like comparing the quality of two prayers? They were two very different people. One was born to dominate, the other was a quieter individual who nurtured a different version of power and happiness. Imrat Khan seemed to have secured the tightly knit, loving family that had eluded Vilayat Khan all his life. There seemed to be respect and love among them, and towards their father. They stayed in close touch. During the two days I was there, Imrat Khan spoke to his son Nishat and face-timed with his daughter Sabiha. They performed regularly together, he and his four sons, in a programme he cleverly titled 'the fifty fingers of Imrat Khan'.

Gharanas and families have unpredictable continnuums. Genes may miss a generation or they may show up diagonally when least expected. Today, the ones who come closest to playing Vilayat Khan's music are neither Shujaat nor Hidayat, but his nephew Nishat Khan and, some suggest, Shahid Pervez, the grandson of Wahid Khan. There is also a musician called Budhaditya Mukherjee whose tonal qualities are reminiscent of Vilayat Khan. Many years ago, his father and teacher had taken some lessons from Enayat Khan in Gowripur. Budhaditya was not sent to Vilayat Khan because his father felt that he would be too daunted to learn. Instead, he learned Vilayat Khan's music from a distance, like an Ekalavya, by listening endlessly, and perhaps more attentively than a student who sits right with the master. Like gorgeous fugues, the music moves forward in different spaces and time zones, with some familiar echoes and many variations.

A family friend recalls a time when, a few years before he died, Vilayat Khan was in Calcutta and Nishat found out. He had to catch an international flight and was running late, but he changed from his jeans into a kurta-pajama and went to meet his bade abba before rushing to the airport.

Is it better to be quietly happy, surrounded by healthy relationships, or to be lonely and famous? These are personal choices. Or maybe they are not even in one's hands. As I was leaving, Imrat Khan said: 'The recordings are already composed for us by the one above. We are just sitting here playing His instrument.'

CHAPTER NINE

Small Loves, Big Loves

Khansahib left Pari Mahal sometime in 1972. But he was clearly done with city life; the next place he chose to live in was equally bucolic and quiet. He picked Clement Town, in Dehradun, a few hours north of Delhi. This is where he spent the next fifteen years.

The period after Shimla and before Dehradun was a time of exquisite sadness. Vilayat Khan's relationship with Imrat Khan had degenerated, and so he lost the one person who had been a source of unconditional support. His marriage had broken down, and Monisha finally left, not on the best of terms. She probably realised that this brilliant mercurial man had never belonged to her and never would. She was competing not with another woman, but an entire universe that made room only for passing travellers.

Vilayat Khan had alluded every now and then to the fact that Monisha was too modern, too outspoken for him. Not too far beneath the veneer of suits, pipes and foxtrot was a man who believed that women should follow one step behind.

In an interview she gave to a newspaper in 1972, Monisha spoke about her marriage. She said that there were certain rules. 'Never scold Donkey (the dog), never raise my voice above a whisper and, above all, never argue. If the Khansahib says "too much salt in the curry", I repeat after him like a Vedic chant, "too much salt in the curry".'

Monisha was not a repeater. She liked the good life as much as her husband did. They were like two competing planets, and their gravitational pulls moved in opposite directions. Before his forty-fifth birthday, she had left.

Perhaps musicians are not destined to have conventional marriages. The lifestyle and the obsessions, the perennial hunger for adulation and applause, the parallel universe they occupy, does not leave much room for normal relationships. Vilayat Khan was away from home for long stretches, and he did not think twice about engaging in short- and long-term relationships. He was surrounded by a legion of beautiful women in Delhi, in Calcutta, in Bombay, in Europe and England—women who were constantly trying to rescue him from himself.

But could it be that Vilayat Khan did not want to be rescued? He had experienced inordinate pain, but he also believed that sadness was crucial to music.

This was also the time when his relationships with his younger brother and his mother were reaching that cul de sac where there was no more room to manoeuvre. These were his oldest loves. It did not matter that he was responsible for the estrangements; they still pierced him to the bone.

He had said in *Komal Gandhar*, 'I have seen a lot of sorrow in my life but all this sorrow that has lived inside me has to come out somewhere, so it comes out in my music. To make others cry through your music, you have to have cried a lot yourself. The music and the tears, they both come from the same place.'

He said there were two or three musicians who always

brought tears to his eyes. His father Enayat Khan, Abdul Karim Khan and his friend, Amir Khan. He wanted to have the same impact on others that they had had on him. Sorrow was not something he ran away from. He embraced it and it glided through his music.

During these difficult times, he accepted friendship and comfort from anyone who offered him shelter from the storm. One such person was the beautiful young widow Naina Devi, a thumri singer who also worked at the Shriram Bharatiya Kala Kendra in Delhi. She adored Khansahib and his music, and believed that a man of his calibre needed to be supported and propped up in every way. Her children were a little unnerved by her blind devotion to this charmer of a musician who frequently stayed in their home in Jungpura as if he were family. But they were equally enchanted by his music.

One of her children remembers a particular evening. After dinner, their mother sat in front of him, making his favourite paan. As she handed it over to him, Naina Devi said, 'Khansahib, why haven't you practised today?'

Without a word, he got up, picked up his sitar and sat down to play. About an hour later, young Billy came running to her mother and whispered in her ear, 'Mummy, come and look!'

She led Naina Devi to the window. On the street below, a small crowd had gathered. They were just standing there, as if in a trance, looking up periodically to see if they could trace the source of this music. It was a sublime moment, because Vilayat Khan didn't know he had an audience. He was just playing.

In 1972 Khansahib met and slowly fell in love with one who would be an immortal beloved. For the first time, it was not a woman.

Satguru Jagjit Singh was a spiritual leader and a musician. He was the head of the Namdharis, a Sikh sect which believes that their gurus did not stop at the tenth—Guru Gobind Singh—but still live among them. He saw strong interconnections between spirituality and music, and firmly believed that if children learned music they would grow up to become better human beings.

Jagjit Singh lived in a village called Bhaini Sahib near Ludhiana in Punjab. It could have been any other sleepy village surrounded by wheat fields except that it harboured an amazing secret: every child was taught Hindustani classical music. Regardless of whether they grew up to become farmers, traders or homemakers, music was their second language. They learned how to sing, play the sitar, sarod, tabla and dilruba. They learned compositions about leaves dancing in the rain, and about Krishna and Guru Nanak. They learned how to accompany each other. They learned how to listen.

The tradition of teaching music to children was started by Jagjit Singh's father, Satguru Pratap Singh, who famously said: 'I want the fragrance of music to touch every child. Music keeps negativity away.' He died in 1959, and his son, who had inherited that passion, kept up the tradition. Jagjit Singh was himself an accomplished singer and played the dilruba, the plaintive notes of which have traditionally accompanied Shabad, the music sung from the Guru Granth Sahib, the Sikh holy book. He didn't want anything from musicians other than for their music to become the air people breathed. Jagjit Singh gradually nurtured a musical environment—in Bhaini Sahib and across India, touching the lives of many non-Namdharis as well. He started connecting with musicians like Vilayat Khan before they became famous.

Musicians in turn admired his rare and pure commitment, especially at a time when classical music was competing with film music and losing the popularity race.

Jagjit Singh recognised the frustrations of young talent and offered them unconditional support and patronage. He once heard a young man sing in Delhi and immediately recognised his potential. The singer was then working as a management trainee at Delhi Cloth Mills. With no hesitation, the guru asked him how much he was earning, and said he would match the amount as long as the man pursued his music. That young man was Rajan Mishra, today among India's most highly regarded singers.

The first time Satguru Jagjit Singh heard Vilayat Khan was on a cassette tape in the early seventies. Enchanted by the music, he sent Khansahib a message through their common friend Amjad Ali Khan, requesting him to play at Satguru Pratap Singh's memorial concert in Delhi in 1972. This marked the beginning of their relationship.

After the concert, Jagjit Singh told Vilayat Khan how happy he was to listen to him and shared a view close to his heart.

'Music takes you closer to God. It inculcates a discipline within you. If your life becomes disciplined as well as lyrical, you will live peacefully. You will not fight with anyone. We will have a more peaceful world. Instead of firing a gun, fire a raga and see the difference,' he said to Khansahib. It was as if he was articulating the musician's own thoughts.

By this time, Vilayat Khan had started viewing the world through a cataract of cynicism. His personal life was denuded; he didn't trust anyone; he was exhausted by the politics of the performing arts world. He felt cheated by the government. But in this astonishing Sikh guru, Vilayat Khan may have seen a mirror of himself and found unconditional love. Jagjit Singh adored the thing that was dearest to Vilayat Khan—his music. Because this was the only language they spoke, Khansahib knew he could trust the satguru, perhaps more than even his family; he often felt there were lurking agendas.

The two of them gradually developed a close friendship. Whenever Vilayat Khan was performing, if Jagjit Singh was in the vicinity, he made it a point to go and listen.

Jagjit Singh recognised the enormity of Vilayat Khan's musicianship and wanted a piece of that magic to touch others. Sometime in the late seventies, the satguru convinced him to come to Bhaini Sahib. That was when Vilayat Khan knew he had found his soulmate.

They spent hours listening to each other, chatting, playing and singing. There was no thought of time or place. Musicians young and old had gathered there. Jagjit Singh told Vilayat Khan how the entire Granth Sahib is set to music. Each verse goes with a raga and there are thirty-one ragas in the book, starting with raga Jaijaiwanti, ending with raga Shri.

Vilayat Khan, in turn, told them stories about music that he had heard, about his father and grandfather and how they could present the entire world in a single note. They shared compositions and made up new ones on the spot. Satguru would sing one line and Khansahib improvised the next one. There was no space for ego, only music and love. Vilayat Khan remarked during one of these musical sessions, 'Here, there is no difference between the ustad and the student. Everyone is equal.'

Jagjit Singh named Vilayat Khan the Namdhari music guru, thus ensuring that he kept coming back to Bhaini Sahib. He also tried to connect many aspiring musicians to Vilayat Khan, and arranged for them to go and learn under him in Dehradun.

One day, while in Jullunder, the satguru met a young Sikh called Virender, a school teacher who was also a good sitar player. He asked the youth who his teacher was, and Virender told him that he had learned from the tapes of a great musician called Vilayat Khan. Jagjit Singh didn't say anything at the time, but a few months later, a messenger arrived at Virender's home in Jullunder and he was told, pack your bags and come with us to Dehradun. He was baffled, but followed them. Jagjit Singh had arranged for him to play before Vilayat Khan, his invisible teacher. When he finished, Khansahib turned to Jagjit Singh and said: '*Saman toh inke paas sara hai, sirf* nut-bolt *theek karne hain!*' He has all the tools, only his nuts and bolts need tweaking. Vilayat agreed to take him on as a student, and Jagjit Singh took care of the fees and expenses. Virender Singh stayed in Dehradun for several months at a time, and eventually became a full-time teacher of both sitar and tabla back home in Jullunder. He also came to Bhaini Sahib and taught the children there.

In one stroke, Jagjit Singh had created both a musician and a musical legacy. He sent many others to learn from Vilayat Khan, sponsoring their travel and stay, and giving them a stipend if need be. At any given time, there would be at least a couple of Namdhari students in Dehradun.

With such interventions, Jagjit Singh was ensuring that Vilayat Khan's music percolated into posterity. He knew that in matters of art and spirituality, the presence of the guru was the key. That is how micro-nuances are passed on, the elements that you cannot learn by reading a book. Vilayat Khan had once told him, '*Diya se hi diya jalta hai.*' A lamp can only be lit by another lamp. He was alluding to an important element of Indian classical music: it has no known beginning and no one knows when it changes along the way. When you listen to an artiste, you may hear elements and influences of past masters, sometimes decipherable, at other times less obvious. A single musician's rendering is like a wave, individualistic and whole when it washes up, but dissolving into a larger ocean when it recedes.

The love between the two men grew gradually, like a tree, sheltering the lives of many who came to sit in its shade. Jagjit Singh had nurtured and loved numerous musicians—Bismillah Khan, Shivkumar Sharma, Amjad Ali Khan, Rajan and Sajan Mishra—but his attachment to Vilayat Khan was special.

People knew that there was something otherworldly about this relationship. During a performance in London, Vilayat Khan threw a tantrum during the interval and said he would not play unless he was paid his full fee right then. The organiser was in a fix. The house was full. It was a ticketed event and people were already getting restless. He suddenly had a brainwave. He made a long-distance call. It was to Jagjit Singh. A few minutes into the conversation, he handed the phone over to Vilayat Khan.

'*Ji huzoor*' is all they heard him say, and the organiser knew his work had been done.

When Vilayat Khan was to perform in Banaras, he was suddenly besieged by that irrational paranoia known to afflict artistes. Banaras was the hometown of Ravi Shankar. Who knows what could happen. He felt foolish sharing his fears with anyone, so he called his beloved Jagjit Singh, who promptly sent two burly bodyguards from Bhaini Sahib, just to be by his side and give him some semblance of comfort.

Many years later, Jagjit Singh sent Vilayat Khan a message that he wanted the two big tanpuras, Vilayat's long-time companions, to stay in Bhaini Sahib. But old habits die hard. Khansahib sent a message back saying that they were not in good shape, that it would cost a lot of money to restore them.

Satguru promptly sent a message back saying, no problem at all, whatever be the cost. Within a few weeks, the money arrived and the two majestic instruments were brought to Bhaini Sahib.

There is a saying in the Sikh holy book: '*Daeda dae laidae thaki pahi*.' You must give so much that the receiver himself gets exhausted. Whatever Vilayat Khan asked for was given without hesitation—money, adulation, love—until Khansahib himself wanted nothing.

Intrigued by this relationship, I made my way to Bhaini Sahib. The village lies a couple of hours outside the city of Ludhiana. I was received at the train station by Balwant Singh, a gentle man with a long black beard, in a white kurta and churidar, whose kirtans I had heard on YouTube. An earthen pot hung from the seat at the back of the car. He explained that he only drank water from a natural source, even when he travelled abroad. His children had never tasted an aerated drink.

As we drove past fields, Balwant Singh told me about the world inside Bhaini Sahib: how they only wear shades of white, the hue of humility and purity; how its children learn ragas instead of watching television. Many of them have grown up and moved to cities like London and Bangkok, but the traditions stay intact and music remains a parallel track in their lives. He also told me about the cherished moments he had spent with Vilayat Khan.

I woke up before sunrise the next morning and was taken to the music room. There, under portraits of great musical and spiritual gurus, sat children of all ages, the girls with their heads covered in diaphanous white dupattas, the boys in white kurtas and shorts. They were learning a rare Vilayat

Khan composition. Some of the children were asked to play their instrument or sing for me, which they did perfectly and in a matter-of-fact manner, as if they had been asked to bring a cup of tea for a guest. The symphony of discipline and devotion made my city-girl hubris slink away.

When it was time for me to leave Bhaini Sahib, I went to Balwant Singh's home to see Vilayat Khan's two tanpuras. The beautiful brown instruments had intricate white latticework which is rarely seen on instruments today. They had his initials etched on them. I touched them and ran my hand over the four strings.

As I got up to leave, Balwant Singh whispered the secret mantra of Bhaini Sahib into my ear, four times as was the tradition. He told me how to chant it—in a loud whisper audible only to me. I felt weirdly secure, perhaps the way Vilayat Khan did in this place where music and love and divinity gently brought about unconditional surrender.

CHAPTER TEN

Roses in Dehradun

Vilayat Khan's days in Dehradun gradually took him from sorrow to joy, for there he embraced new love. In 1975, when he was forty-seven years old, a baby boy came into his life like a ray of sunshine. His new wife—whom Khansahib had transformed from an unassuming, barely educated Lisa into Begum Zubeida in keeping with his fabulous imagination—gave birth to Hidayat. The little boy, with his father's aquiline nose, became a beautiful distraction for a man whose love for children was no secret. Shujaat, Yaman, Zila and 'Bayboo' Hidayat became his little props of joy, now all at ages where he could enjoy them, engage with them and, of course, ignore them at his will.

Lisa, some twenty years younger than Khansahib and completely beholden to him, slipped into the role of the comforting consort he so desperately needed. She did not question him. Nor challenge him. She cooked great food and looked after the children. She walked one step behind her husband, and quietly learned to press the buttons that gave him solace.

Once again, an even larger extended family filled with

students, tailors, entertainers, maulvi sahibs, servants and random relatives filed in and out of the house. Khansahib liked to have people around him constantly.

He bought the house and named it 'Surbahar'. It was nothing special as a structure, but the interior was opulent, almost like the home of a zamindar and not a sitar player. It was filled with chandeliers, oil paintings and exquisite Persian carpets which had been gifted to him by Farah Diba, the queen of Iran, whom he had taught briefly before the revolution. On one of his trips to Tehran, he had found half a dozen priceless carpets rolled up and left beside his luggage. When he went to thank Farah Diba, she also handed over a small white pistol which he carried with him until he died.

The rose garden in front of the house was Vilayat Khan's great joy and he spent many hours pottering about there, humming to the flowers. On one side of the property, there were sheds for cows and buffaloes who had names like Nani and Dadi. He had ducks called Laila–Majnu, and dogs called Musky and Poppy. His favourite creature was a rooster who, he proudly told everyone, crowed every morning in raga Pahadi.On another side of the house was the badminton court. He insisted that the children do something outdoorsy and sporty every day. Indoor games included monopoly and cards; there was no question of watching television.

Visitors would be housed in various pockets of the property depending on a hierarchy decided by Khansahib. Musicians like Amjad Ali Khan, Bismillah Khan, Amir Khan and Ali Akbar Khan stayed in the main house. Staff and students stayed in the outhouse.

Besides music, food was a big obsession. During his travels across the country, if Vilayat Khan happened to eat a particularly delicious dish, he went into the kitchen, spoke to the chef and invited him to Dehradun. A feast would then be arranged on the terrace or the backyard of Surbahar to celebrate the chef's cooking.

Khansahib needed to be constantly entertained. Either there were card players on hand or other randoms—like his children's dance masterji whom he invited to come and stay to amuse him and his friends at night, dancing to popular film songs of the time, especially ones featuring the actress Rekha. When they had all sat down after a meal, he would tell the children and students stories from his travels. He spoke animatedly about the exotic food that was served in the palaces of Iran and Afghanistan. Between students and family and the constant visitors, Khansahib was never deprived of an audience.

'I will never forget the meals I had with King Zahir Shah,' he told them one evening, in the mood for nostalgia. 'I was getting ready to leave because I wanted to be back with all of you, to celebrate my birthday. I was turning forty. When the king found out, he refused to let me leave. He didn't give me a choice. He took me to Karez-e-Mir, a beautiful town in the Hindukush mountains where they had a smaller palace. And there he told the cooks to make forty different exotic pulaos and ensured that I tasted each one of them before I took off. And for my birthday he gave me hand-crafted rifles. What a time it was!'

Through all this colourful noise, music remained the constant undercurrent. It kept him from tipping over. And Vilayat Khan was always joyous when a musical friend visited him in Dehradun. He was particularly ecstatic when Amir Khan came and stayed for several weeks.

Early one morning—it must have been around six, for the sun had already risen—Shujaat woke up to practice. It was usually a time when everyone was asleep, because Khansahib and his coterie drank late into the night. Shujaat shut his eyes and started the haunting lower notes of raga Bilaskhani Todi.

Just when he was reaching the komal rishabh, caressing

it with tremendous care, the door opened and a six-foot-tall figure stood silhouetted against the morning light. It was Amir Khan. Shujaat was about to stop and get up in deference, but the older man gestured to him to continue playing. He walked in and sat there quietly, listening attentively, in his signature posture—one hand on the mattress, the other resting on his lap. Shujaat couldn't see the expression in his eyes because of the thick lenses set inside his black spectacle frame. His face was sombre, like that of a sage.

After fifteen minutes, Amir Khan asked Shujaat to stop and said, 'What are you playing?'

'Bilaskhani Todi, Chachu.'

'Who taught you this?'

'Ji, Abba taught me.'

He thought for a minute and then looked at Shujaat with a little smile. 'Does he know? Of course he doesn't know. He only plays the sitar ... Come on, let me show you.'

He sat with his eyes shut and back erect, the way he did on stage. He started singing Bilaskhani Todi, building on notes in the lower register in that unhurried meditative manner that no one else could do before him or after. He was demonstrating the Merukhand technique of building a mountain of melody, gradually and with great mindfulness, without any desire to titillate. It was as if he was a solitary presence in the room.

One of Vilayat Khan's students, Jung Singh, had been watching this encounter from the threshold of the room. He immediately went and woke Khansahib up.

'Abba, please come. I think something is going to happen in that room.'

Khansahib got up, rinsed his face, and came to his son's room, his white muslin kurta still crumpled from sleep. He sat down on the floor. Jung Singh sat down next to him. By now, two or three other students had emerged from various corners of the house and crawled into various corners, to watch this unexpected masterclass unfold. Vilayat Khan signalled to one of them to get his two tanpuras. He stepped out of the room to tune them.

By around eight in the morning, which was usually the time that the scent of freshly watered grass mingled with the aroma of parathas simmering in ghee, the music was in full swing. Shujaat was playing his sitar seated on the floor, attentively following Amir Khan, who continued to sit on the bed in front of him, lifting his hand to direct him. Jung Singh played a tanpura on one side of the room. The other tanpura was being played by Vilayat Khan.

Everyone sat respectfully, facing the great singer, as if in a temple of music. Cups of tea floated in, and empty cups were refilled at least two times over—the session went on for the next three hours, until the notes of the majestic morning raga had serenaded the entire house, drifting out into Surbahar Avenue, touching the rose petals, and lingering for many hours even after it was all over.

Later that evening, Amir Khan and Vilayat Khan were chatting over their whisky about the meaning of riyaz.

'I remember that Abba used to tell me that I need not practice ten–twelve hours a day,' Amir Khan said. 'He used to say that technical perfection is only half the game. The other half is thought. The musical imagination has to be active.'

Vilayat Khan had heard about how Shahmir Khan would contradict the norm of the times and make his son practice only three times a day, for an hour at a time. He nodded in agreement.

'Bhaisahib, will you sing Hamsadhwani for me? Please, my soul needs it. I will play the tabla, chalo.'

And Amir Khan started 'Jai Mate Vilambe', one of the compositions that eventually immortalised him. He was slurring slightly, and after the first verse, they both ended up laughing.

Left to right: Yaman, Hidayat, Vilayat Khan, Lisa, Zila and Shujaat

In the evenings, Khansahib would often ask all his children and students to sit with him, and he played records to them. That particular evening, it was Ella Fitzgerald singing the Blues.

'Listen to her voice. Listen to the way she sustains the notes. It may not be Indian classical music. It may not be ours. But it has its own beauty and resonance and we must all learn from it.'

There were many such moments when unlikely voices broke the routine of raga music. Anyone cycling past Surbahar late at night would have been startled to hear the sweet sultry voice of Ella or Janis Joplin, or an aria by Mozart or Bach. Vilayat Khan's all-time favourite was Bella Bartok, the Hungarian composer. These were not musicians he had grown up hearing, and yet he was drawn to them and brought them into his world with great openness and humility.

But the music he listened to for hours on end was that of the old Indian greats—Zohrabai, Kesarbai, Faiyaz Khan, Abdul Karim Khan and Omkarnath Thakur. He had all their long playing records. He made his children and whoever was around him listen with deliberate awareness.

'Listen, listen. Just listen to the way Kesarbai has hit the upper rishabh in Todi. See her sense of balance. See her emotion. Her pukar, the way she throws her voice. Learn from it. Learn from it ... People applaud me for creating the gayaki style and the five-note meend, but I think I did all this because I could not play like them, like Enayat Khansahib. Compared to his music, my sitar is like a single bell on an anklet. You all did not have the good fortune to hear him, but listen to as many greats as you can.'

After the piece was done, he would play it again. And then again. This is how he swallowed each note and phrase until it flowed in his blood and emerged in some form in his own music. He could replay any of the pieces any time from memory. If someone were to lift the needle of the record somewhere in the middle of a piece of music, he could sing the precise phrase or note that was going to come next.

'Children, there are four great singers who have influenced me and I want you to learn what is great about each one. Faiyaz Khan was royal and regal and dignified. Abdul Karim Khan represented beauty. Bade Ghulam Ali Khan was about freedom. He was like a bird who could take off from a tree, fly anywhere and land exactly where he wanted.' He then paused and put both hands in front of him, palms close to his face as if he were praying. 'And Amir Khan is only about ibadat. Prayer.'

A few weeks later, he got the news that Amir Khan had died in a terrible car accident in Calcutta. He was sixty-two years old. Even though Zeenat and he were now divorced,

Amir Khan's body was brought to the Park Circus house for the last rites. Vilayat Khan didn't know it then, but thirty years later, he would be laid to rest a few feet away from his friend so that their souls could still hum to each other.

Late one night in April, Khansahib was practising raga Lalit, even though it was a morning raga. Arvindbhai's daughter, Purvi, who used to learn singing from him on and off, was in Dehradun. She and Zila were seated on a vast turquoise-and-pink Persian carpet, listening quietly, giggling softly among themselves.

Suddenly, the lights went off. No one flinched, for power outage in these parts was as common as the hill birds. The maestro didn't stop for a second. By and by, someone came in and lit two candles. The flames threw a quivering halo around the musician. In that shadowy space, the music sounded even more sublime and seemed to rise to another level, causing all human existence to diminish and fade out. The absurd anxieties of life seemed to disappear. Conversation was redundant. And the two madhyams of the raga, so subtly intertwined and yet distinctly separate, started up a brilliant dialogue.

The next morning, Purvi got up early, hoping to carry on the magic and perhaps learn something new from him. She peeped into his room, but he was not there. Nor was he in the main living room, sitting on his favourite armchair. He was not to be found in the house.

'Lisaji, where is he?'

His wife smiled and pointed towards the driveway. 'He has been there for the last hour.'

Purvi stepped outside and saw a pair of legs sticking out from under the Mercedes.

'Khansahib, what are you doing?' Purvi asked.

The musician crawled out and stood with his hands on his hips, staring at the vehicle in front of him. Then, he answered thoughtfully, 'Baby, you know where the stepney is? If we remove it from there, we can keep more luggage in the back. I have figured out a way to create a clamp on the outside where the spare tyre can be fixed. That way, we create more space inside.'

He had decided that he wanted to change the vehicle's configuration so that it would carry more people as well as more luggage. Khansahib spent hours tinkering with the car until he came up with this solution. He also decided to add more shock absorbers, so that the entire car lifted up and looked like an absurd version of itself.

Purvi stared at him in disbelief and realised that this was not going to be a morning of music. He had entered another space. But he was as engaged with the car, tuning it with complete concentration as if it were a musical instrument. She shrugged. Amazement had come to be a routine response to this extraordinary and unpredictable man, this human alloy of multiple talents.

Sometime in the late 1970s, Satguru Jagjit Singh and a group of music students from Bhaini Sahib arrived in Mussoorie just to be close to Vilayat Khan. They booked an entire hotel for a week. The seven days merged into seven nights, and were filled with music, laughter, philosophy and food. The singers Rajan and Sajan Mishra, who had been discovered by Jagjit Singh, were also present. The guru's student Balwant was there, and Khansahib's young children would fall asleep listening to the music.

On the last night, as they sat together, they could have been two philosphers from a distant past, changing the way the world might think many centuries later. Jagjit Singh's fingers moved silently on his white rosary beads. Across the carpet was Vilayat Khan, in his usual white short-sleeved kurta, with self checks. Fifteen or twenty others sat around, all devotees of music.

'What was so great about Enayat Khan? And about Abdul Karim Khan?' said Vilayat Khan with a dramatic flourish. 'It was that they could offer that innocent, simple, truthful note—it was so perfect that they made it sound almost impossible. That is because they themselves were simple. We need to recall that simplicity. We complicate our lives needlessly. All the complexities we see around us are actually a reflection of what is within us. We're always fighting. It's almost as if we are fighting with ourselves.' He jiggled his body, as if to demonstrate many internal demons.

Jagjit Singh smiled. 'Seeing is one thing, vision and focus are a completely different matter,' he said.

'Absolutely true!'

'You know that story of Arjun and his teacher Dronacharya,' Jagjit Singh continued. 'All the young warriors were being taught how to aim and focus. On the day of the test, a clay animal had been placed on a wood platform. Everyone was asked, do you see this clay animal? They answered, yes. Do you see the dog next to him? Yes. Do you see me? Yes. All of you can leave then. The guru then asked Arjuna, can you see the animal? Yes. Can you see anything else? No. Shabash. That's the definition of focus. Then you are on your way.'

'Aah, what a beautiful story. So it's better to be like an obsessed lover than a distracted worshipper,' said Vilayat Khan. 'Now let me tell you a story. A Majnu was walking around dazed, muttering his lover's name, his feet blistered, but he was oblivious. He passed by a maulvi sahib who was kneeling in prayer. The man suddenly got up and slapped the Majnu and said, "How could you just walk past me while I was reading the namaz?" The Majnu said, "You saw me? While praying? Well, I never saw you!"'

Satguru smiled.

'Who was more focused here? Who was more in tune? What you see, what you don't see. It is very important.'

'Wah wah!'

'Whenever I see you, Satguru, I feel better for months. You are my ruler, my pir, my king, my lover, my friend … I don't need much else. If I have your love, I don't need any certificates or prizes from the government. This is what makes me happy. This, and picking up my sitar or singing when I am alone.'

As Jagjit Singh was leaving, Vilayat Khan said, 'Satguru, you know that you are my mashuk, my lover, and I am yours. Come on, say it!'

Jagjit Singh laughed and they hugged each other.

A year or two later, the two of them met in the home of the musician Trilochan Singh in Delhi. After they had all greeted one another and sat down to chat, Vilayat Khan once again said, 'Come on, you have to say you are my ashiq and I am your mashuk. We are old loves.'

Again, Jagjit Singh just laughed.

Vilayat Khan said, 'If you don't say it now, I will take my life.' He jumped up. 'I will take my life by banging my head against this column until I bleed to death.

Jagjit Singh responded, '*Kabool kabool kabool!*'

In Dehradun, Khansahib had a constant stream of students staying with him. He treated them all the same, scolded them and loved them and taught them the beauty of the sitar. Some were also taught the tabla, so that they could keep time with him when he was practising. Yaman often sat as his rhythm-keeper, terrified that she would miss a beat because it was so easy to get distracted by his music. The young girl's trick was to focus only on the rhythm and block out the melody.

In the early eighties, on one of his annual trips to Kolkata, Vilayat Khan had heard two young boys play the sitar in the home of a student. He found out who they were and met the father of one of the boys, Debashish.

'Will you send these two boys to me in Dehradun?'

The man hesitated and looked at his feet.

'What are you worried about? My fees? Don't even think about it. I am not interested in the money. These boys have great talent. After they are done with college and graduation, leave them with me for a few years. I will change their lives.'

Some months later, armed with back-up academic degrees to ensure that they would always find employment in the real world, both boys arrived in Dehradun. They were welcomed warmly by Khansahib and Amma, which is what Lisa became to everyone in her husband's life. Their music training began right away, and they soon merged into the routine of Surbahar.

The very next day, Vilayat Khan sat in front of all his students and said, 'If you practice twenty out of twenty-four hours, you will be a great sitar player, but you will have nothing to differentiate you from the others. All your concerts will sound the same—brilliant, perhaps, but not memorable. Not the kind of music that can make your audience cry one minute, smile the next, and be completely taken by surprise the very next moment. So, you have to not only sit with the instrument, but constantly think about it, about the music. That way, not only will you enjoy the music more, but so will your listener.'

There was complete silence. The only sound was the musical chime of the bird outside.

'Listen. Just listen to that pakhi—how she has hit the right notes, from madhyam to shadaj. Be that bird ... sing, fly ...'

In the evening, he pushed all the children to go outside and play badminton. If they said they were tired, it was not tolerated. The very young Hidayat was the one to protest the most and get reprimanded the most.

'What do you mean tired?' Vilayat Khan growled. 'This is part of your training. When we were young, in Saharanpur, your great-grandfather Bande Hasan Khan and all the musicians would go every morning, right after the first call to prayer, to the akhada where they would wrestle to build up their stamina. Pah! You children have no idea what it takes to be disciplined.'

It was badminton some days, kabaddi when the weather was good. Sometimes he would join them, be the referee or play a game with them.

At night there would be some card-playing, or Khansahib would sit to practise. And everyone would sit around, listening, talking, until it was time for bed. One of the students or children would then go and sit with him while he fell asleep, pressing his feet or his back. Sometimes he would ask for a story; he specially loved children's stories. They lulled him to sleep. Late into the night, he would be gently snoring, when suddenly his fingers would start moving rhythmically, pulling on imaginary strings, and then his head would move slightly, as if a magnificent composition was swelling inside his dream consciousness, silently preparing for when it could emerge. These kinds of moments happened very often when he slept, whether in the afternoon or at night. The music never stopped.

One day, all the students had gathered in the big room for the usual morning practice. But instead of practising, they were fooling around, taking turns imitating all the great musicians, making fun of the way they sang and played and contorted their faces.

Suddenly, Hidayat nudged Debashish. Vilayat Khan was standing at the door, frowning, his eyes bloodshot, his face filled with rage.

'Who do you think you are? Not only are you not doing your own riyaz, but you are making fun of the elders in our field who have done their riyaz and become great musicians.'

The children were mortified that a little prank could elicit such an angry reaction.

'Your punishment today is that you will not get lunch.' He bellowed out to his wife, 'Amma, please make sure you don't give them anything to eat until they have sat and practised till their fingers are numb.'

No one spoke a word after that. There was only music and frenetic strumming in over-appeasement mode. Finally, a little after two in the afternoon, Amma came and said, 'Come, eat.'

'But abba said no, we are not allowed to.'

She paused and said softly, 'He hasn't eaten himself. He is waiting for you. Come on now, it's okay.'

They went silently to the dining table, heads hanging, still a bit terrified. Khansahib was sitting at the table. He looked around at the penitent brood that sat before him.

'You children have to understand. These great masters, these pandits and ustads, have done so much work, it's unbelievable. You are all babies still. You are in no position to make fun of them. Of course, I too have made fun of people and mimicked them. That is why, along with you, I have punished myself. I have not eaten either. Come, let us all eat together.'

Debashish was on the verge of tears, ashamed and moved and inspired at the same time. All the others looked mournful. Seeing their expression, Abba said, 'Okay, the lesson is over. Let me tell you what a prankster I can be.'

He then told them the story of how a young tabla player from Delhi had called him and said he was going to visit Mussoorie, and would like to drop in and see Khansahib on the way. Vilayat Khan never appreciated being by-the-way. He waited patiently for the man to come. After tea, he told the visitor, 'Don't bother taking your car. My son will drive you to Mussoorie in our jeep. You are our esteemed guest.' He took Shujaat aside and said, 'If this man reaches Mussoorie, I will break your legs.'

They proceeded along the winding road, and a few miles down, poor Shujaat stopped the car and said there was a problem. He took it to a mechanic and waited while nothing was done. The musician sat around and was finally told that it was getting too dark for them to negotiate the hill roads and they were better off turning back. That was the end of his trip. Vilayat Khan, of course, greeted him with warmth when he returned, and no one said a word about anything.

'So, children, you see, I love mischief too. But I never let it come in the way of music. If your heart is not in your practice, don't bother sitting there. Stop playing, get up and go indulge your distracted mind. Then come back and sit. With proper devotion.'

Among the sundry characters that hung around Surbahar was Nazeer miyan, a tailor who came from a family of impoverished musicians. He could be heard humming long-forgotten compositions while cutting beautiful silks and shaping them into kurtas and shirts for the maestro. Sometimes Khansahib would sit with him and cut the cloth himself, showing Nazeer exactly the look he wanted. This will work with this, and this colour will work better with that. The buttons should be at a particular distance from each other, and offset the fabric. Under his supervision, the tailor transformed from a crude maker of ordinary clothes into a haute couturier. Khansahib also spent hours sitting with Farid miyan, the fabric man who arrived every few months from Lucknow, bearing bales of cottons and silks.

Vilayat Khan took great pains over his attire and appearance. In fact, before every concert, he insisted on a complete dress rehearsal, for which the entire household would be prodded into action. He would carefully select his clothes depending on the occasion and season and mood ... the kurta had to be ironed just right; the shawl that would cover his feet while he played had to be matched; even the jewellery he wore was laid out on a side table, in perfect alignment: the watch on the left, the silver chain on the right, the ring exactly in the middle, the handkerchief in a corner. If someone changed the placement of any of these things, there would be an irrational outburst.

The night before he left for a concert, his silver paan box was also properly set, because this too went everywhere with him. He had designed it with great care to contain a bizarre medley of items: his mizrabs or plectrum, a small pen which he had sawed to fit into one of the compartments, small beedis which he always prefered to cigarettes and smoked in private, and the various ingredients that went into making a paan. The box would open from both sides. On one side, a maze of compartments contained these sundry items. The bottom opened into the part that housed the fresh paan leaves.

This was the ritual before he was ready to drive off for

a concert in his Mercedes—every single time. In Delhi, he liked to stay at the India International Centre, preferably in the same room.

He had to prearrange everything, God-like, especially when it came to public performances—but even otherwise. He used to practice even the deliberate, almost impaired, way he walked on to stage, building up towards the image of a maestro. He detested musicians who left things to chance, to sudden inspiration. Khansahib carefully planned his public appearances—the combination of ragas, down to the number of minutes he would spend on the slower alaap, the speedier jhala, and how best he could conclude the show with a light piece so that the audience left smiling.

The dress rehearsal applied as much to the children, if they happened to be attending the show. 'Your behaviour and dress must always have melody in them,' he said. 'They must be appealing.' They had to select and wear their clothes the night before, parade in front of their father and get his approval.

'This is a bit too loud for Vilayat Khan's daughters to be seen in,' he said to Yaman who, like any pretty, attention-seeking teenager, kept veering back to her bright orange or pink kurtas.

'Try that outfit Nazeer miyan made for you, the white-on-white one. It is much more becoming for girls to look modest and low-key. And please, you know my views on this—strictly no make-up.'

The two girls looked at each other from the corners of their eyes and swallowed their teenage sniggers, for their father's wrath was not something anyone could handle without some heartbreak, even after years of trying.

One day, Khansahib asked Yaman to get him a glass of water. When she brought it to him, he took one look at her hand and gently pushed her away. She was taken aback.

'But, Abba ...'

'It's okay, I'll get it myself.'

'But, Abba, what happened?'

'Nothing.'

'Abba, please, please don't do this to me. I know you are upset. Please, please tell me what I did.'

'Your nails. How many times have I told you I don't like to see long nails on my girls?'

The young Yaman sobbed in her room that night. Through her tears, she remembered the episode over her passport picture in London. She had cheated and worn lipstick for the picture. Her father looked at it, looked at her and said, 'Sorry, you will not travel to Amsterdam with us.' And she was left behind.

The children knew that they had to make a choice between their individuality and their father's love, and this remained a tussle for the rest of their lives.

It wasn't easy for the young women who, apart from normal teenager angst, were already coping with a host of emotions that came with an estranged mother, a new stepmother who had once been the very person their mother had ordered around, and a loving but supremely autocratic father who was always there but not there.

It would have been hardest for Shujaat, a young man coming into his own as both man and musician, to deal with a father who wanted his firstborn son to be like him—but then could scarcely deal with another Vilayat Khan. A series of casual clashes had begun to put pressure on their relationship until it finally blew up.

By now, Shujaat had started taking his music more seriously and needed no push to practise. He had experienced the headiness of performing in public, and had already travelled on his own to a private island in Seychelles, where the Shah of Iran hosted a group of talented young musicians, seeking to get children's perspectives on music.

In 1974, when he was fourteen, Shujaat accompanied his father for the first time—to Berlin. Vilayat Khan had been invited to spend four months teaching and performing at RIAS, Radio in the American Sector, a liberal radio station which promoted world music. This was the time Shujaat started getting close to his father. It was just the two of them, there was no one else around to distract his father's attention.

When they got to the airport in Delhi, Vilayat handed the tickets to his son and said, 'Come on, check in.' This would be the first in a series of instructions that would prepare Shujaat for the life of a travelling global musician.

When they got to the hotel, their German hosts had arranged a lavish suite so that father and son could be together. Vilayat Khan, however, had different plans. He said his son was now old enough to have his own room, and it would be better if they had their own separate ones. Shujaat smiled inwardly; he knew that his father's desire for an independent room was not premised on facilitating his son's freedom, but his own.

Shujaat had started getting a sense of how to cater to Western students and audiences. While Vilayat Khan taught, he'd have Shujaat demonstrate—how to practice, how to start a performance.

One afternoon, while they were both relaxing in the hotel, Vilayat Khan gave Shujaat some money and told him to go down the road and buy biscuits. He returned with a brightly painted tin. They both popped a biscuit each into their mouth and then simultaneously spat it out. Vilayat Khan picked up the tin and, below the undecipherable German, saw the picture of a dog with a ribbon around its neck. He burst into laughter.

'Shujaat miyan, these are dog biscuits!'

One misty November morning in Dehradun, Vilayat Khan called out to Shujaat, as usual expecting him to drop everything and come with him.

'Take the car out. Let's go do some household shopping.'

'Sure, Abba!'

The two of them got into their red jeep and headed down the road. At the crossing a little further down, the road forked into two—one towards Dehradun, the other towards Saharanpur.

'Make a left here.'

'A left? Why do you want to go this way? I thought we were going to get things for the house from the Dehradun market.' Shujaat shuddered inwardly at the thought of going to Saharanpur and meeting the relatives who fed him the best biryani in the world but also talked endlessly.

'Just listen to me, Baba.'

Shujaat knew better than to argue and continued down the hill road, a bit confused but aware that his father had a destination in mind. About half an hour later, his father asked him to pull up in front of a large grocery shop. Seated behind the counter was a young man and an older couple. As soon as they saw Vilayat Khan, they jumped up and ran out to touch his feet.

Khansahib started rattling off his list—rice, wheat flour, three different kinds of dal, onions, oil ... Then he introduced Shujaat to them.

'This is my elder son.'

'Khansahib, why didn't you bring him before? So nice to meet you. Adab.'

Shujaat was a bit baffled by these acquaintances. He asked the young man if he could use the bathroom, and was ushered into the house behind the shop. There, bigger than anything else in the living room, was a portrait of his father, smiling down from the wall. On either side were pictures of the usual collage of gods and goddesses that find their place in Hindu homes.

Shujaat was astonished. 'So you really like the sitar?' he asked the older man who had escorted him in.

'Not really.'

'But are you a fan of Vilayat Khansahib?'

The man smiled sheepishly and said that he didn't really understand music. By then, Vilayat Khan himself had walked in with the younger man, chatting and laughing.

The man said, 'Khansahib, you haven't told him our story? He knows nothing of our relationship.'

Many years ago, when the teenaged Vilayat lived alone in Delhi, and often didn't know where his next meal was coming from, he had met this man at a railway station where he ran a small tea stall. For some reason, the man had reached out to the skinny boy. He fed him, gave him some money and told him that he could come to his house whenever he needed anything. In the course of their chats, they discovered a Saharanpur connection and the bond was further cemented.

Twenty years later, Vilayat Khan went back to look for the tea stall but it was not there. He managed to locate the owner and learned that he was suffering from tuberculosis. Khansahib took him back to Saharanpur, paid for his treatment and bought him the shop. He filled it up with things that would sell easily and got him back on his feet. That was over ten years ago, but he had never talked about it to anyone in his family.

Shujaat drove back in silence. He was still digesting the

side to his father that he had just seen. It made him suddenly empathetic towards the hardships his father had been through as a child, something he could scarcely imagine, having grown up in reasonable comfort. His father's stories about poverty and cold weather and those days when he would cycle to Deobandh to play in some dusty mausoleum for a few rupees suddenly seemed more real. Backstories can change the filters of perception. They never talked about that encounter again.

Most people who knew him realised at some point that, for everything that could be said about Vilayat Khan, the opposite was also true. He may have been flamboyant and self-obsessed, but he could also be deeply compassionate as random strangers would find out.

Every Ramzan, he would go back to either Saharanpur or Etawah or Calcutta, places where he had some roots and where there was still some family, and participate in a wildly generous act of charity. The poor would be fed food that they would not even be able to dream about for the rest of the year; he would insist that they be given his favourite dishes, like sweet chicken pulao and mutton kofta biryani. The old and infirm would be treated to otherwise unaffordable cures and surgeries. The daughters of poor widows would be married off and get new lives. One year, when the government launched a scheme to set up public call offices, Khansahib paid the deposit for several young men who were the children of unemployed musicians. And after one of these magnanimous acts, the inscrutable Vilayat Khan would once again retreat into his self-absorbed, decadent, crazy world and shut the little wicker gate with a sign that clearly said: 'No entry beyond this point'.

By the time Shujaat was in his mid-teens, father and son were like periodically clashing cymbals, the resonance of which lasted long after an uproarious fight. It was a relationship of profound ambivalence, not uncommon between two strong male egos, complicated further because it was a father–son bond that was both nurturing and destructive.

It was when they travelled together, and were away from the shroud of family, students and acolytes, that Shujaat and Vilayat Khan bonded. Like their time in Berlin, or a few years later, when they travelled together to New York, the first time for both.

On the one hand, he was being groomed by his father.

On the other, he was trying to break free.

The family had already been fractured by the divorce, and the constant back and forth that the children had to do in their growing years. While the older three adored their baby brother Hidayat, there was also a tinge of envy at the attention he got from having both parents around. Teenage years are difficult at the best of times and a broken family only compounds this. A father who alternated between being autocratic and absent did not help. It is likely that, because Shujaat had the brilliance as well as the charisma of his father, the friction between these two very strong personalities continued to grow.

Khansahib often used his loyal servant, Kareem, to send messages to Shujaat, to upset or humiliate him. Shujaat finally took his revenge, leading his siblings into grand rebellion, using poor Kareem as his missile.

It was holiday time. Khansahib was travelling and would be meeting them in Bombay. The children were about to leave Dehradun, and were all bundling into the car to leave for the station. Shujaat called Kareem aside and pointed to his father's most prized botanical possession—the rose garden in front of the house.

'You know these roses? Abba is tired of them. He felt very strongly that they should be uprooted and we should grow rice paddy in their place. And the bungalow is looking so drab. He wants it painted blue. Kareem, please do all this before we are back. He will be so pleased with you.'

The servant obliged.

Shujaat was a lot like his father—hot-headed and honest. He did not like being controlled. He had to get away to figure things out in his head. In his late teens, Shujaat left home and travelled across the world. He left his music. He partied at discotheques. He moved into the Divechas' apartment in Bombay as a paying guest. He dated many women. Every once in a while, he played at a concert.

When Shujaat got married to Parveen, a lovely young woman of his own chosing, the entire family accompanied the young couple on their honeymoon to Chail in Himachal, and made a grand holiday of it. Vilayat Khan adored her. But then a shift started taking place. Gradually, he began indicating that he did not approve of his daughter-in-law's family. It is likely that politics within the family started coming into play—first-family and second-family issues. Shujaat had to make choices. One night, after a card game in which Vilayat Khan was, as usual, indulging in a naughty old habit of cheating to win, Shujaat threw the deck on the table and left the Dehradun house with his bride, never to return.

It was an important musical moment, for Shujaat Khan had to break away from the shadow of his legendary father to become Shujaat Khan. He went through the grind like many artistes do, as rites of passage. He travelled on cheap overnight buses to concert venues, withstood his father's wrath and taunts, suffered haughty patrons, and practised and performed, and practised and performed. The world tried its best not to give him a space. The music world can be political.

If Vilayat was playing somewhere, then Shujaat wasn't likely to be called to the same festival. Despite everything, he slowly established himself as one of the top-billed artistes in the country.

The strange thing is, he didn't really play Vilayat Khan's music. Even today, many do not even know that he is the son of Vilayat Khan. Shujaat once said, 'He wanted me to be exactly like him, but then couldn't deal with another person like him. I have his touch, his blood, his feelings, his emotions, but my own personality.'

At some point, the profoundly ambivalent relationship between them settled into an enormous, though mostly unspoken, mutual respect between two wonderful musicians.

I went to meet Shujaat in his lavish 'farmhouse' in Chhattarpur, the posh suburb of Delhi where many modern nawabs opt to live, to be away from the grime of the city. During the years that he was in and out of Delhi, travelling on the international music circuit, Parveen had set up their home. It was beautiful, overlooking sprawling gardens, one of the best in the neighbourhood. They had two children.

Shujaat was relaxing in a white kurta-pajama, handsome and rotund. He was between trips to Dubai and America. But he was reluctant to talk about his father. Here was another lid that had been closed. Now an outsider was prying it open and the contents could boil over. But I cajoled and persisted. And what emerged was a story rife with equal helpings of beauty and pain, and gradual resolution.

'You know that the children of a genius either become drug addicts or dwarfs. It is impossible to grow under the shadow of a giant banyan. It doesn't let the sun in,' he said.

'I knew I could never be better than him. The balance, the control, the raga, the emotion—everything about him was superhuman. And yet, when we played together, he gave me a footing on stage. He acknowledged that I was also there. He never suppressed it. He allowed me to be. Our playing together was never bitter, it was always sweet. Because it involved me watching him up close, seeing his genius and trying to match his genius, and getting those spontaneous appreciative wah-wahs from him—which was great.'

This brilliant and articulate man had figured his way out and planted roots of his own. He had created a personal and professional life that few artistes of his generation had. Shujaat was a genuine celebrity. Every once in a while, a Delhi socialite would offer to pay him just to make a guest appearance at her party, so that the hosts could appear culturally cool.

While Shujaat built his own life and career and kept a healthy distance from his father, they were both professionally smart enough to also do concerts together over the years, because they made for a compelling duo. Their music and their emotions did not cross paths. No one in the audience would guess there was strife if they did not already know of it.

But Shujaat kept his wife and children away. He did not want to expose them to his father's whimsical ways. Perhaps it was also his way of getting back at a man who he knew loved children.

The last time that they played together, the audience may or may not have heard it ... This was a concert at the National Centre for the Performing Arts in Bombay. It was a tiny moment that could have gone unnoticed. And yet, sometimes a moment can project an entire lifetime. Vilayat Khan turned to his firstborn and said, '*Motu, tumhari bari.*' Fatso, go for it.

CHAPTER ELEVEN

Bhairavi in America

It is possible that Ravi Shankar's embedded presence in the United States was why Vilayat Khan was loath to touch American shores. He was close to fifty when he gave his first concert in New York in 1978, strangely, thanks to the department store Bloomingdale's.

In the seventies, an inventive retail tycoon called Marvin Traub decided to transform a dowdy department store into an upmarket chain. He started exposing his customers to unique and exclusive merchandise from all over the world, which they wouldn't find anywhere else, and created eye-catching window displays and visible branding. Bloomingdale's shoppers were treated to products from Israel, China, France, Italy and the Phillippines. But the most incredible promotional exercise was the one on India, which brought some thirty dancers, musicians, artists and craftsmen to the United States. Vilayat Khan was one of them.

It was an enormous project: Bloomingdale's coopted Air India, India's flagship airline, to host a poster competition among Indian artists. The winning image, a flying elephant, was printed on over half a million shopping bags and store catalogues. Parts of the store were dressed up like Indian bazars, featuring life-size papier mâché camels painted in bright colours and covered with little mirrors. The store wanted to create a spectacle.

Vilayat Khan was flown in on Air India in the summer of 1978 as part of a concert series under the banner 'India: The Ultimate Fantasy'. Although he was initially reluctant, his friend, the film director Ismail Merchant, convinced him to do it, and the money was good. Shujaat, who was eighteen and aching from his first heartbreak, accompanied his father on the tour.

'Don't worry son. There are so many women you still have to meet,' was his father's advice to him as the plane took off.

The concert series featured Vilayat Khan at Jordan Hall in Boston, where he also gave a lecture demonstration at Harvard University, and at the National Museum of Natural History in Washington DC. In Los Angeles, he got a standing ovation, according to a review. The show-stopper was at Alice Tully Hall at the Lincoln Center in New York City. He was accompanied on the tabla by Avtar Singh, one of the Bhaini Sahib students, and Shujaat played along with him after the interval.

The New York Times wrote:

> One does not have to have an intimate familiarity with the sitar to realize that his flawless rapid-fire interval jumps, downward-arching glissandi and hammered notes in pearl-like clusters are the work of a musician who has mastered his instrument ... At times he strummed across the sitar's entire fingerboard like a flamenco guitarist, only to resolve the rhythmic tensions he created with evanescing unexpectedly placed glissandi. The dynamic peaks and valleys in the performance were carefully controlled and, as a whole, maintained an admirable sense of form and proportion.

Vilayat Khan did not return to the US for nine years. He moved briefly to England in the middle, and performed in London, Paris, and across Europe. During this time, he made a few more enemies. That seemed to be what he did when he was not playing music. As one family member said, 'He emotionally manhandled people! If someone so much as whistled at him, he would pull out his gun.' The big fight in this case involved a host of musicians, including his estranged brother, Imrat Khan.

The BBC had asked Vilayat Khan to curate its annual Proms series in 1981. It was an all-night concert at the Royal Albert Hall, starting at 11 p.m. and finishing at 7 a.m. the next morning, with three intervals. The other musicians were the sarangi master Sultan Khan, vocalist Niyaz Ahmed Khan and, on the surbahar, Irshad Khan, who happened to be his nephew. Avtar Singh and Zakir Hussain were the tabla accompanists. Vilayat Khan himself concluded the performance.

As always, the point of contention was money, for there was a discrepency between the amounts that Vilayat Khan had negotiated with the BBC and the actual sums the artistes eventually received. When they found this out, some threatened not to play, others protested that they had been unfairly treated. Cool as a cucumber, Vilayat Khan justified his stand by saying that he was playing the dual role of musician and event manager, so he deserved to make some money. But he also reportedly remarked, 'And anyway, I'm the one who taught Irshad everything he knows.' When Imrat Khan heard this, he was livid. Zakir Hussain reportedly threatened not to accompany Vilayat until the money matter was sorted out. Not one to be outdone, Vilayat turned to the young tabla master right in the middle of the concert and said: 'You know how to count pounds, now let's see you count your taal.'

These years were spent travelling back and forth between London, Dehradun, Calcutta and Bombay. But Vilayat Khan had sampled the love of America, and was possibly waiting for an opportunity to go back. He finally returned to New York in 1987 on the invitation of the World Music Institute, an adventurous music promotion organisation started by an Englishman in New York. Robert Browning was the very painter who had once been touched by Imrat Khan's music on BBC radio many years earlier.

Browning had since moved to New York and become one of the first promoters of world music concerts. In the mid-1970s, he had started sourcing and presenting unusual music from all over the world at an art gallery in Soho. The first performance was by a group from Ecuador. He also found a local sitar player from Queens called Diwan Motihar to come and play. These were the first in a series of shows that piqued the curiosity of an audience that was clearly bored with American pop. People lapped them up, the concerts became more frequent and, by 1985, Browning established the World Music Institute with a small grant from the New York State Council. Hordes of inquisitive young people would find their way to these small concerts. Local music critics from *The Village Voice* and *The New York Times* started paying attention by writing detailed reviews and applauding the new initiative.

Browning soon discovered that Indian classical music attracted a mainstream audience more than any other world music. 'Initially, the audiences for Indian music would be 75 per cent South Asian and 25 per cent American. Over the years, it became 50–50, including second-generation Indian-Americans, especially if a crossover star like Zakir Hussain was playing. In comparison, at Persian music concerts, the audience was almost 85 per cent Iranian-American,' he said. Browning believed that Ravi Shankar and the Beatles and Yehudi Menuhin were responsible for this.

In 1986, Browning invited Vilayat Khan to play in Carnegie Hall, but Khansahib was unable to make it, so he featured Nikhil Banerjee instead. The World Music Institute hosted its first Vilayat Khan concert in 1987 and many more subsequently. Even though his shows were never house full—unless Zakir Hussain was accompanying him—Vilayat Khan was Browning's favourite Indian artiste 'because he was not flashy and didn't show off on stage'.

When Vilayat Khan returned to America in 1989, he did a thirty-five-concert tour across the country—featuring at the Kennedy Center in Washington DC, Carnegie Hall in New York, as also Florida, Los Angeles and San Francisco. He was accompanied on the tabla by Gobindo Bose for the first half of the tour and by Zakir Hussain later.

This time, his younger son Hidayat accompanied him and Khansahib tried to make him sing in between, but the teenaged boy was mortified, and after the first concert, begged to be let off the hook.

It was at a World Music Institute concert at Alice Tully Hall in New York in 1989 that a young photographer called Lyle Wachovsky first met Vilayat Khan. He came to the green room afterwards with two friends—Misha Schreiber and a young tabla player called Badal Roy who, when he was not playing with jazz musicians in Harlem, worked as a server at the Pak-India Curry House in midtown Manhattan. Lyle kissed Vilayat Khan's hand as if he were the Pope and told him how much he adored the Jaijaiwanti he had just played. He told him how Misha was one of the most well-regarded tabla teachers in New York, and how they would attend every Indian classical music concert they could catch. That night, he drove the maestro home and, on the way, invited him for lunch the following day to Misha's home on Manhattan's Upper West Side.

Misha was thrilled at being able to host the great sitar player, and cleaned and tidied her home the way she did just before Passover. She had learned many delicious Bengali recipes, and decided on a chicken korma and dal for that day.

Lyle followed Khansahib around as he performed across the country, in Buffalo, Detroit, San Diego and San Francisco. He became his fan-boy, his chauffeur and a ready ear. After the San Diego concert, he was driving Khansahib to his host's house late at night when Vilayat said, 'Lyle, I am hungry.' It was past midnight and nothing was open, but Lyle was determined not to disappoint him. Circling around endlessly, they finally reached Denny's and had two beef burgers each.

By the time they reached Los Angeles, Lyle had won Vilayat Khan's trust. He convinced him to sit for a recording in a professional studio. Vilayat Khan named his price—10,000 dollars, all cash. Lyle agreed and instantly booked Sun Studios. The equation was clear: Lyle wanted the music; Vilayat Khan wanted money.

'Raga Bhairavi,' declared Lyle.

'But there will be no tabla, so shall we do only alaap?' Vilayat Khan asked.

'Give me a few hours, Khansahib,' Lyle replied. He made a few calls and found Shamal Bose, a tabaliya who happened to be in Los Angeles and happened to be free that morning.

'Just one request, Khansahib.'

'Tell me, Lyle,' said Vilayat Khan who, by now, had begun to like this man who loved him and his music so unconditionally.

'Please don't do any of the scale changing you usually do. No masti. No mischief. I want the pure stuff.'

'Ah Lyle. I like the way you say masti!' he laughed. Vilayat Khan agreed to comply with the request, surprised to find such a purist in an American who had no background in Indian classical music. He also admired the absence of fear and hesitation in him, and his straightforward professionalism, so unlike the Indians he had encountered back home, where there was always unctuous adulation and over-the-top displays of respect, but no one could really be fully trusted.

He played an hour-long Bhairavi. It was the recording that inspired the creation of an incredible music label, India Archive Music.

By the time they returned to New York, Lyle was a man in love. He had just read an interview in *The New York Times* in which Vilayat Khan spoke about music in a manner he had never before encountered:

> 'Our music became systemetized thousands of years ago,' Mr Khan explained by telephone from Bombay. 'Through the notes, musicians found colors and effects: cool notes, hot notes, combinations of notes that represent the seasons of the year or the hours of the day. One gives the effect of the monsooon; one is dry, like powdered snow; some are red, as in the sunset; some are red as in the sunrise. All these notes have a particular effect and colour, and it is from these that ragas are built ... Yes, it is a very complex kind of music, and listeners in your country may not understand all the details. But you know, the right note, the right sound, is something that everybody understands.'

It is baffling how the son of a Jewish immigrant who fitted glass windows developed such a love for Indian classical music, but Lyle decided that he wanted to spend all his spare time sourcing and recording Indian musicians. A few months later, he learned that a group from the Sangeet Research Academy, the reputed conservatory in Calcutta, was touring the United States. The musicians were being led by the Academy head, Vijay Kitchlu, also a singer. The group included Girija Devi, the gorgeous semi-classical singer from Banaras, the sarod player Buddhadev Das Gupta, and two upcoming singers who had just started making a name for themselves—Ajoy Chakraborty and Rashid Khan. He followed them on their concert tour and then convinced each of them to record for him in a studio in New York.

Lyle was now a man possessed. He decided to travel to India and continue recording musicians there—Debashish Bhattacharya, Tejendra Majumdar and Dhondutai Kulkarni. In 1990, he recorded Shujaat Khan as well as Imrat Khan in New York. By then, he had sufficient material to launch the India Archive Music label, a collection of pure classical music, which deliberately stayed away from light music, chanting and cover titles like 'Scintillating Sounds of India' or 'Royal

Ragas'. This was pure raga music and the sleeve cover designs were straightforward, featuring photographs of the artistes shot by Lyle. India Archive Music's only competitor at the time was a company called Raga Records run by another Jewish New Yorker called Ira Landgarten—also coincidentally a photographer obsessed with Indian music. But there was an unwritten understanding that they would not publish the same artistes.

Lyle knew that just presenting the music would not be enough. Americans needed to understand what was being served to them. 'When I first discovered this music, I remember finding a rare Ali Akbar Khan album by World Pacific Records which explained the alaap in thirteen parts. It gave me a handle on the music,' said Lyle. 'But that was a one-off. Most of the time, it was merely "we're improvising" and we had to make do with that.'

He started looking around for someone to write the sleeve notes and discovered Deepak Raja, a perfect choice, for he both understood music and was an accomplished writer in English. Their friendship grew because both were equally enamoured of Vilayat Khan, and spent many hours on the phone discussing his rendering of a particular raga.

For the first time in the history of recorded Indian music, the albums carried extensive sleeve notes detailing the minutiae of what was being played or sung, analysing the raga, the gharana and the artiste with academic precision. 'I wanted copious notes because I wanted to give people more knowledge. People in the US had no idea about this music, they had not grown up with it,' Lyle said.

But after all his musical journeys, Lyle's heart pined for Vilayat Khan. He knew there was something there that no other musician had. Lyle did not feel the same way about Ravi Shankar, whose name had become synonymous with the sitar. Besides, he would not be able to afford him.

Lyle took a deep breath and made the decision. He would invite Vilayat Khan to come back to the US and sponsor his stay for six months. He would organise concerts for him across the country. Then, he could record Khansahib endlessly and satiate himself. This would be his life's main mission even though he knew the risks it involved. It had long bothered him that there was no quality control on what was being freely passed around in the name of Indian classical music, much like chicken makhani and naan.

In 1989, Lyle rented a small house in Somerset, New Jersey, an hour away from New York City, and handed over the keys to Vilayat Khan, Lisa and Hidayat. He also arranged for a young tabla player called Akram Khan to fly in from Delhi. The fees were fixed and there was no going back. By the last recording, he was paying Vilayat Khan 12,000 dollars per sitting, all cash.

It is unclear how Lyle funded his music business. The first lot of albums were not bestsellers and the concert halls were at best half full. Some whispered that he had funders from the Russian drug mafia; others said that he had made some money on his own. It didn't matter. What emerged over the next six months were some of the best recordings of Vilayat Khan ever, captured on state-of-the-art equipment at the historic Astoria Recording Studio in Queens. With a top-class sound engineer called David Merrill, and the 48-track NEVE board with multiple microphones, the studio could have recorded an entire symphony orchestra.

Lyle believed that an artiste performed better when he had an audience, so he invited music lovers to sit in on all his recordings. Afterwards, they would order tandoori chicken and parathas from a hole-in-the-wall Indian restaurant on 37th Avenue in Queens and there would be a little party in the studio. Lyle said that Vilayat Khan was a pure professional and everything would go smoothly, start to finish. 'He knew the drill.'

Every few days, Lyle brought paan from Little India on Lexington Avenue and spent the day with the Khan family in Somerset. If Khansahib wanted to go for a spin in the car, he happily obliged. They became close, and soon 'Khansahib' became 'Abba'. Vilayat Khan had two sources of entertainment—aimless long drives and shopping. He would spend hours pottering around the supermarkets, examining the mind-boggling varieties of produce and meat.

'Lyle, what is the difference between the mutton priced at 9 dollars versus the one that is 12 dollars.'

'It's the quality of the meat, Abba. Just that.'

'Ah, well, I will buy the lower priced one and Lisa will cook it so that it will taste better than the higher priced one.'

Sometimes they would drive around aimlessly and get lost. But the carpets of fall leaves and the little lakes along the way made Khansahib happy.

'Lyle, where are we?'

'We're here, Abba.'

'Okay.'

It may have been the fifth or sixth session when Vilayat Khan played what may be one of his most extraordinary pieces of music, one that didn't sound the same when he played it before or after. It was a raga he had invented called Sanjh Saravali—a beautiful variation of raga Yaman Kalyan with a touch of raga Bihag. According to Deepak Raja, 'the 78-minute bada khayal style rendition of this raga, recorded for India Archive Music, New York, will qualify amongst the greatest pieces of instrumental music recorded in the post-independence era.'

It was not as if Vilayat Khan was a bestseller like Ravi Shankar. On his coast-to-coast concert tour during those six months, the halls were never packed, and Vilayat Khan would be quick to blame it on weather conditions. India Archive Music must have sold some 20,000 or 30,000 CDs over the years, which would scarcely cover the cost of production. But Lyle didn't care. He believed in Vilayat Khan.

I met the intriguing Lyle Wachovsky in New York. He had a white beard and twinkling eyes. We instantly became friends and went to eat sushi at his favourite Japanese restaurant on the Upper West Side. He told me about his days with Vilayat Khan or Abba, and imitated the way he used to say 'Lyyyyle' in his slow deep voice. He was charming and mildly grumpy.

Later, Lyle and I went for a drive along West End Avenue, a beautiful stretch that runs along the edge of Manhattan, adjoining the Hudson river. We stopped at a corner, next to a magnificent Gothic church. It was a beautiful spring day and the trees were in full blossom and there was a happy New York state-of-mind vibe in the air—people of all ages and colours roller-blading, walking dogs, jogging, writing poetry by the river. Lyle stopped the car, turned off the engine and played a recording of Vilayat Khan's Shankara.

'Listen to the way in which the taans tinkle. It's as if fairies are dancing all around us.'

We also listened to the stunning recording of Sanjh Saravali. 'I love the other pieces, but this is the one I enjoy the most. It's very special. I remember that, in the car on the way to the studio, Abba and Hidayat were singing the composition, but when we started the recording, I requested him to stick to pure sitar and he didn't argue. Then, it all came together, in one take. It was extraordinary. No other recording of the raga has ever been the same.'

He spoke with utter reverance and I realised what an

extraordinary contribution Lyle had made to the music world. Many years ago, Dhondutai, my music teacher, had spoken about one 'Lyle' with great regard. It must have been around 1990. She was not a popular artiste and yet, unlike most brazen Indian record companies who used to humiliate her by quoting unacceptably low fees, he had not once bargained. This was the first time a music label had given her such respect. Lyle admired her pure, uncompromising style. Her recording remains unpublished—along with a hundred hours of recordings—including Vilayat Khan's Bilaskhani Todi, Bhairavi, Khamaj and Basant Mukhari and a rare one of him playing Kafi Kanada on the surbahar—which Lyle hopes will gradually find their way into the market, once he can raise the money.

Music travels in non-geographical realms. Around the same time that hippies and groupies like Misha and Lyle were being touched by Indian music in the West, many Indians back home were being influenced by jazz or rock and roll. It was as if there was a silent exchange taking place, invisible luminous beings moving from one continent to another, bringing people closer and reminding them that there was something greater than their individual selves. We all live under the same sky.

How did a man who had no connection with India come to so obsessively archive its music? His only connection to music was that his father used to play jazz records in their Washington Heights apartment when he was a boy. As we drove back, Lyle made me promise him that if I came across any old recordings which were lying around in some forgotten drawer or with a dying collector, I would ensure that they didn't just get lost. These were priceless heirlooms, he said. I was ashamed of my own indifference to such things and, moved by his unremitting enthusiasm, reassured him that I would.

CHAPTER TWELVE

Portrait of an Older Musician

By the time he was in his sixties, Vilayat Khan's temper and rancour had become legendary. People almost expected him to begin his concert with a lament against the government or a tangential reference to a certain popular sitar player.

Even when he was at the top of his game, he felt a conspicuous disenchantment with the music scene in India. In the late seventies, he had a particularly unpleasant experience with an audience in Bombay. He was performing at Shanmukhananda Hall in support of the Naval Charities. The hall was packed with dignitaries, including Governor Ali Yavar Jung, Admiral Nanda and the singer Kishori Amonkar.

Khansahib was in a great mood, laughing with friends and fans who popped into the green room where he sat making his paan. A woman wearing a headscarf appeared at the door and said a salaam. Vilayat Khan looked up at her and smiled. '*Tum aa gayi ho.*' You have come. Her eyes smiled back at him, and then she disappeared into the auditorium. She may or may not have been one of the many fireflies who flickered briefly in his life.

The concert began on a good note, with Khansahib playing a flirtatious Hamsadhwani. About an hour into the concert, sounds of people coughing and clapping in the wrong places emerged from the gallery above. The disturbance did not stop and it was soon clear that this was some malicious disruption, not the usual apologetic coughing that punctuates concerts. Suddenly, in the middle of a taan, Khansahib put down his sitar, got up and walked off the stage. The curtains hurriedly came down. A few minutes later, the governor came on stage and reprimanded the audience. Kishori Amonkar got up from her seat and requested the audience not to leave. But there was no sign of Khansahib. Finally, he came back with the governor and spoke tremulously.

'I am deeply hurt and I would like to be excused from playing the rest of the concert.'

Vilayat Khan left and went straight to Arvindbhai's home on Altamont Road, where he was staying. He sat quietly on the balcony with Arvindbhai and stared for a long time at the Mangalore-tiled roof of an orphanage, which would soon after be pulled down to make way for a tower to house India's richest family. No one voiced it, but everyone suspected that the disturbing elements that evening had been planted by a rival's groupies, almost certainly without his consent or knowledge.

Vilayat Khan spoke softly. 'I am feeling more and more disturbed about living in India where there is such little appreciation for our culture. Today I am very, very sad, Arvindbhai. I am very, very sad.'

The music climate in India at this time was one in which many great classical artistes felt an unbelonging. Film music had become the predominant score. The passionate patrons who used to adulate classical musicians, secretly record them and covet the presence of these artistes in their homes, were a dying breed. In their place were concert organisers who relied on sponsorships and constantly had an eye on ticket sales. Popularity was integral to success. Bureaucrats made arbitrary decisions about awards and funding, and the music world was rife with politics.

In contrast, audiences in Europe and America were growing more enthusiastic about Indian classical music. While a concert in India would pay Vilayat Khan among the highest rates, he could earn far more in London or Europe. Around the same time, a Hindi film playback singer would have been making several times the amount a classical artiste was paid.

Vilayat Khan once said in an interview that film music and All India Radio's overemphasis on light music 'had corroded tastes'. He said that there were any number of glossy magazines dedicated to film stars, but not even one devoted to classical music and to making artistes more popular.

It is likely that this uninspired climate pushed many Indian classical musicians to Europe and America, where they often found second wives, second careers and many adoring students. By this time, the Ali Akbar Khan School in California had become an enormous success. Zakir Hussain moved to the same area. Ravi Shankar lived in Los Angeles and started a school of music there. Many artistes found their way to Germany and the Netherlands where they were welcomed.

In the late 1980s, while he was on tour in America, Vilayat Khan met his old friend Ali Akbar Khan in California. They cooked together and sat up the entire night chatting and sharing stories. Ali Akbar knew that there had been a problem with the Dehradun house and that his friend was very troubled with family issues.

'Vilayatbhai, you should also think of moving here. These people love our music and the money is good. It will take you away from all the problems at home.'

The decision was not too difficult.

The final trigger in Vilayat Khan's decision to move was a sinister incident in Dehradun. Crime in Uttar Pradesh was out of control and an industrialist's son had been kidnapped for ransom. Vilayat Khan's family had also received a couple of threatening calls. One evening, Hidayat and some of his friends were driving home along the forested slopes when a jeep overtook them brutishly, and suddenly they saw a hand come out of the window and shoot a gun into the air. It may have had nothing to do with Hidayat, but when Vilayat Khan heard about it, he made the decision.

His short stay in America had been rewarding. He liked the pace and ease of life that he had seen. He also felt that the US would be a more conducive environment to raise the young boy, who was then fifteen. His older children were all married. Basheeran Begum had died in 1986. This time, he started the paperwork to make a more permanent move to the US. As always, he had friends and fans in high places and was immediately assisted by the office of Daniel Patrick Moynihan, the former US ambassador to India, who adored Vilayat Khan's music.

In 1991, he rented a house in Baltimore, Maryland, with the help of some distant relatives who lived there. This is where they stayed for a year or two, moving back and forth between Baltimore, London and Calcutta. Dehradun was a closed chapter. Now that they no longer had access to the Park Circus house, Vilayat Khan bought a flat in Hastings in Calcutta, in a building that the residents reverentially renamed 'Sitar'. With summer in America and winter in India, Vilayat Khan settled into a routine of teaching and performing.

But the shadow of Ravi Shankar remained, and in America he made a valiant attempt to differentiate himself by emphasising that he was a purist. In an interview with a newspaper around that time he said, 'Tradition should be modern but only to the point that it does not lose its identity ... If there are chairs in my room, should I give up sitting on carpets?'

Around this time, he was performing at the Kennedy Center in Washington DC. While Hidayat was doing the sound check, a distinguished-looking man with snowy white hair stood in the wings and listened. When Hidayat was done, he walked on to the stage and introduced himself.

'I am Isaac Stern. Your instrument sounds lovely. I plan to come and listen to Vilayat Khan this evening.'

He sat through the concert, in the front row. Afterwards, the two maestros met and chatted about all kinds of things, from music to the Gulf War.

That is when Stern said, 'Why don't we try and do something together?'

Vilayat Khan paused and then spoke very deliberately. 'Isaac, when one colour mixes with a second colour, you do get a third colour. But my music has always been about going deeper into what there already is, rather than going laterally into new territory. There's enough to explore in this music and many lifetimes are not enough to master that.'

Without actually saying it, he was seamlessly dismissing the music and collaborative creativity of Ravi Shankar. He paused and then continued. 'Besides, I don't want to compromise or mediocritise either your music or ours. That is fusion confusion. It would help neither Western classical music, nor Indian classical music.'

Isaac responded with the same quiet respect. 'What you are saying is 100 per cent correct. I couldn't agree more.'

Vilayat Khan said, 'You know, India's art and music have thousands of years of history behind them, reflected in the teachings of our saints, in the carvings in our temples. They are not matters of fashion. We must have the courage to tell the West, "You should study us and we should study you". Let us not be swept off our feet by superficialities, otherwise the sitar might go the way of the Spanish guitar.'

Stern got up and embraced Vilayat.

It has been said that when he gave concert performances, Vilayat Khan's grandfather Imdad Khan used to restrict himself to playing two ragas—Puriya and Yaman. And if he was performing, no one else dared to touch either of those ragas. If anyone questioned him, he would say, 'Even one life is not enough to get into these ragas. We have to keep going deeper. There is no end.'

In 1991, Vilayat Khan had a massive stroke. He was in Delhi at the time. It is possible that family tensions conspired with years of excesses to bring it on. It started with a bout of bad hiccups. By the time he got out of hospital, his speech was slurring and the left side of his body was paralysed. It was an enormous blow to a man who had cultivated his public appearance so carefully. His hand would now tremble and he couldn't play his sitar for almost a year. Khansahib lost his confidence; this was the first time that he was not in control. This was the man who used to be able to walk on to stage, grab his audience by the collar and with the very first stroke of his sitar say: 'Sit down and listen to me. For the next few hours, I own you!'

But Vilayat Khan gradually and miraculously managed to transform his music to suit his new state. He changed the way in which he tuned his instrument. The result was that when he played a note, it was no longer a single note but a chord. This gave a whole new depth to the music. It was like transforming a water colour into a textured oil painting.

Vilayat's communication with his audiences became more intimate, he talked to them, he sang more in between playing, and people loved him even more than before. Besides, his approach to playing became far less aggressive, the manner in which he struck the joda–chikari changed, and the music that emerged had a new, measured maturity.

He mellowed down easy, finally playing music the way he wanted to play it. There was contentment. In one of his recordings at this time, he played only the slow alaap. It was a non-commercial decision that did not fit the paradigm of what was expected of an instrumental performance. But he no longer had to prove anything.

By this time, Vilayat Khan had tinkered so much with his instrument that it became a sentient being. It was alive. It had become sensitive to all of his inputs and responded to him with feeling. Wherever he went, Khansahib would tap the wood and see what was going on with it, how it sounded that day, how it was responding to the temperature and the environment. He would check his instrument's mood.

The stroke didn't merely impact his music. Vilayat Khan's entire demeanour started changing. He became less obsessed with his appearance, allowing those decisions to be dictated by comfort over style. He didn't go crazy if his kurta was not starched and ironed to creaseless perfection. The earlier Vilayat Khan would not have been caught dead in track pants or pajamas, but he increasingly spent time in a short-sleeved vest with loose white pajamas. He was now mostly bald, with a halo of greying hair. It is likely that his sexual restlessness also abated.

The biggest impact his stroke had on Vilayat was that there was suddenly an urgency to teach his beloved son Hidayat everything he knew. He bent all his energies to focus on a boy who was in his late teens and had just been pulled out of a sleepy, happy life in Dehradun and thrown into a new country. Hidayat did not have a firm base he could call home. He had to pick up and leave every time his father felt fidgety and needed a change of environment. Today it was Baltimore, tomorrow it could be Calcutta or Bombay. While on the one hand it meant enormous exposure, on the other it was a life of no fixed address. He was not entirely comfortable around Americans. And he couldn't bear the Indians who hovered obsequiously around his father. He also had to be on call at the drop of a hat for an enormously entitled, highly renowned musician. With all this going on, Hidayat would have to find his moorings himself.

As for his identity, that had already been determined by birth. He was meant to carry forward a great legacy. And he couldn't succumb to a state of the ordinary.

One of the most terrifying things for a child is to be born into a powerful tradition where expectations overrule individuality. What followed over the next few years was a very difficult relationship between a domineering father and a reluctant student. The gap between them spanned not just ideologies but a difference of almost fifty years. There was love, there was respect, but there were many cross-communications that led to bitter fights, slammed doors and long periods of silence, while a helpless amma watched from the sidelines.

Almost every morning, there would be a row over the fact that Hidayat had not woken up for practice. Abba would ask for his son. Amma would run to his room and find her beloved boy under his blanket, raising five fingers, begging for a few more minutes of sleep. She also knew that he had been out late with his friends the previous night. She was torn. If he didn't wake up, there would be more shouting, more unbearable silence. Her son's happiness was at stake. Her husband's health was at stake.

One day, Hidayat refused to get up until noon. His father

was waiting for him, face like an angry thundercloud. 'You are useless. Get out of the house,' was all he said. And Hidayat did. It was the first of many times he left home.

One evening, in the mid-1990s, Vilayat Khan was teaching a very reluctant Hidayat raga Puriya.

'Abba, can I please go out and meet my friends? We already made the plan.'

'You cannot go, Bayboo.'

He said it quietly, without looking up from his game of solitaire. He was sitting on the bed, playing with his old deck of cards. Hidayat sat on the floor in front of him, seething, playing the sitar, thinking only about what he would rather be doing instead.

'Keep developing the part between ni and ga,' Khansahib said. He demonstrated some movements and then asked the young man to do them on his own. Hidayat did not show his irritation, he continued playing, finding different ways to tackle the four notes.

About half an hour into this, without looking up from his cards, Vilayat Khan said, 'If you are bored, be bored, but don't get up.'

Hidayat was ready to kill his father, but he continued to play the sitar.

It was while father and son were on a concert tour in Oregon in 1997 that Hidayat felt a small shift take place in his music—and his father heard it too. They had played together on stage. Because of the angle at which he was sitting, Hidayat had been able to closely observe his father's right hand modulations and saw how he extracted so many different tonal textures from the instrument. That night, when he was back in the hotel room and his father was in the shower, he pulled out Vilayat Khan's sitar and started playing, paying attention to minute differences in tone.

Vilayat Khan emerged from the bathroom with a look of utter joy on his face. He knew his son had seen the music. All those years of berating him, arguing with him and persisting had paid off. His towel still wrapped around him, abba sat on the bed and started talking to Hidayat in Urdu, with the quiet enthusiasm that comes from finally having found a discerning audience.

'You know, there used to be this Persian carpet in our house. If you brushed the carpet one way, it looked exactly the same. But if you brushed it the other way, you could see a slight difference towards the very end. It was so, so subtle that you might not even notice. You had to look carefully to tell the difference ...'

Hidayat put his sitar down and sat cross-legged, resting his chin on his knuckles, listening intently. 'Bayboo, the carpet was created by a master-weaver, but he died midway and the last bit was finished by his son. Obviously, the way the two men held the thread must have been slightly different. But that minute difference is what you need to get into your music. Pay attention to that level of detail. If you have that kind of eye and vision, then people may not consciously realise what you are doing, but on a subconscious level it will transport them and grip them.'

Vilayat Khan reached into his suitcase and pulled out a deep red Kashmiri Jamawar shawl covered with paisleys. 'Look at these patterns. If you go close, each one looks so intricate, and when you look at it from afar, it is a totally different experience. It's the same with a Rembrandt painting, blurry up close, but when you move away, it all comes together. You have to put that into your music. In the pattern of a taan, the difference between the first phrase, the second phrase and the third phrase is so minute that until you complete the entire taan, you don't see the full picture. Suddenly, when the taan is coming to an end, the full picture emerges and it feels so defined, so complete.'

Vilayat Khan got up, kissed his son on the cheek, and then proceeded to turn on the television. A World Wrestling Federation game was in full swing. He watched it to the end of the fight.

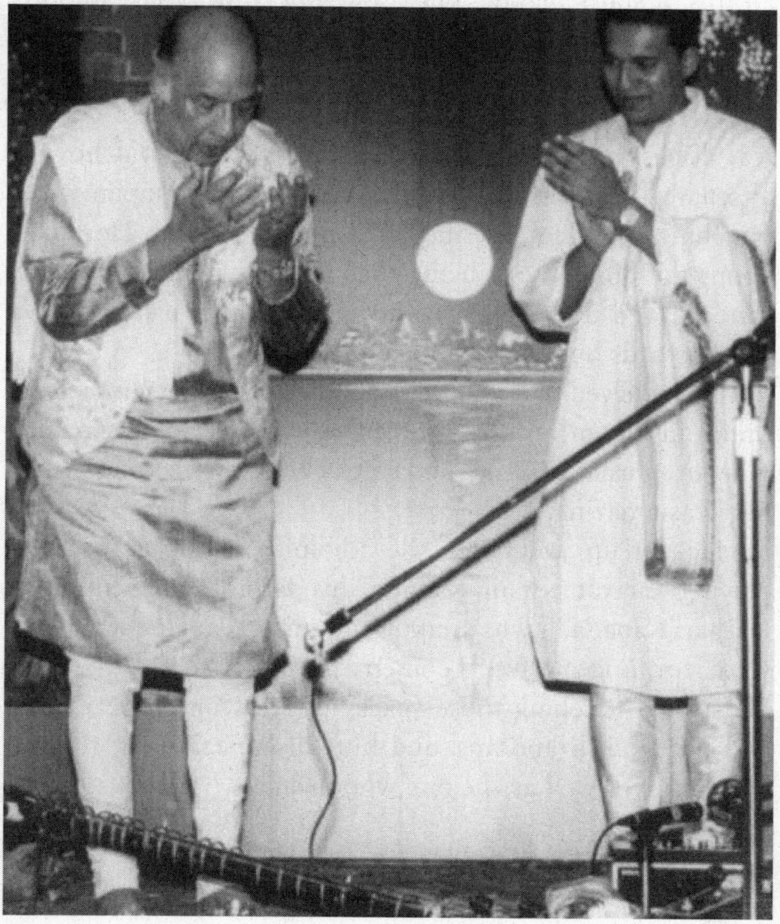

'I now realise what he was teaching me, almost thirty years later,' says Hidayat. 'If you're given such a small space to work in—basically four notes—you learn to be innovative within the boundaries. You are bored out of your mind, so to fight the boredom, you gradually start finding different mathematical movements. You find another movement, and then another. And then, when you are bored of the melodic movement, you start exploring a change in the tone or in the texture, or how much weight to put on the notes. After you have done all this, it starts making sense and you realise that you have all this stuff to choose from when you actually perform. It all makes sense now ...'

Hidayat and I spent many hours, over endless cups of tea, discussing his father. He told me stories about how he alternated between son, student, chauffeur, accompanist and punching bag. He described the incredible love. He talked about the difficulty of being the son of a genius with great candour and deep empathy, not just towards his father but also towards himself.

'He believed that you must develop an interest in the finer things in life, in beautiful design. All that eventually reflects in your music ...' said Hidayat. There was a long pause. 'He was amazing.'

He got up, went into the adjoining room, and started playing Enayat Khani Kanada, his father's reinvention of Darbari Kanada. It was evening and small triangles of sunlight were forming perfect geometrical patterns on the wall. He started touching those spaces where wings spread open and boredom evaporates and hurt disappears—for the one who plays as well as the one who listens.

When Vilayat Khan left Baltimore for good, a part of his old self was back in action. At the airport, the family checked in their luggage, but his hand-crafted Paxman leather sitar case remained with him. He sat with it by his side, chatting with the entourage that had come to say goodbye. It was getting time to move towards security check, and Hidayat kept looking at his watch and prodding his father.

'Abba, we are going to miss the flight if we don't go this second,' he finally said—an exasperated plea. Their names were being called on the public announcement system. Abba finally got up, in a grand slow gesture, and picked up his sitar case. By then, one of the airline's ground staffers had come to find them.

'Sir, sorry, but you will not be able to carry the instrument on board the flight.'

'Sir, sorry, but without this, I will not board the flight.'

Another staffer showed up, visibly irritated with these dawdling Indian passengers.

'Sir, that is fine. We will offload your bags.'

By this time, Hidayat was clearly livid with his father's antics, but he could not say anything in front of the others. Amma was quiet.

The attendant went to the computer to find the passenger's details and looked momentarily horrified. Flashing on the screen in front of him was the information that fourteen bags would have to be identified and taken off. The flight was due to take off in twenty minutes. She spoke to her colleague, and they went up to Vilayat Khan, who was looking particularly handsome that day in a black turtleneck and grey blazer.

'Sir, please proceed.'

He got up, winked lightly at his friends, and started walking towards security.

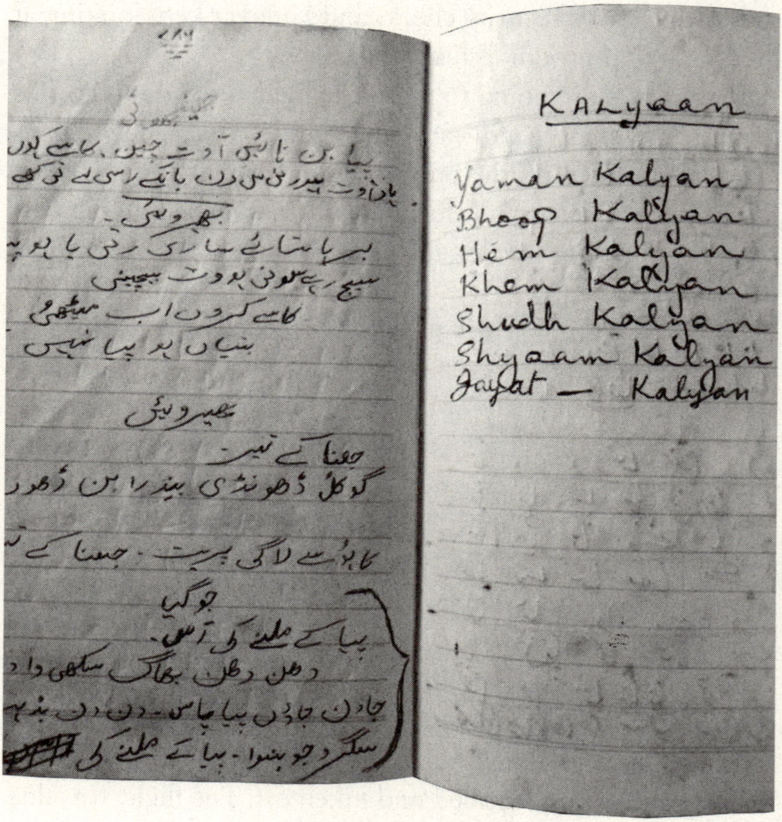

KALyaan

Yaman Kalyan
Bhoop Kalyan
Hem Kalyan
Khem Kalyan
Shudh Kalyan
Shyaam Kalyan
Jayat — Kalyan

CHAPTER THIRTEEN

Princeton Walk

Princeton is a pretty little town, about an hour south of New York. It is home to one of the world's finest universities and it is also the place where Einstein once lived, with periwinkles growing in his front yard.

Vilayat Khan's decision to move to Princeton had nothing to do with the university. He moved there because he loved the unmanicured beauty of the place, the tall maples and elms that changed colour every season. While he was in Baltimore, he had spent some time with friends who lived in Princeton, Renu and Praful Shah. They convinced him that it was a most salubrious environment. So, when they found him a house in a quiet gated community called Princeton Walk, where squirrels and ducks could be his daily companions, he was happy. He had always loved animals and trees. Besides, by this time, he had grown truly tired of human interaction and pointless conversations. 'The lake next to the house clinched it for him,' recalls Renu Shah.

He moved to Princeton Walk in 1993. But he continued to return to Calcutta for a couple of months every year. Just before the trees lost their leaves and a silent sheet of powdery white covered everything, he would go back to the place where the morning call to prayer evoked raga Bilaskhani Todi and all was well with the world.

While his earlier life had been a series of super-fast taans, this phase was like a meditative alaap. He slowed down and retreated into a life that was almost boring. Possibly for the first time, he could be what Americans call 'a regular guy', for that state of ordinariness had eluded him from the time he was born. Here, he didn't have to be the son of Enayat Khan, or 'the mercurial musician', or the 'legendary Khansahib'. At sixty-five, he could finally slip off his persona and relax a bit. Anonymity gave him levity. He spent hours pottering around in the supermarket or at Home Depot picking up little do-it-yourself tools, or at the local textile store, giving in to his old sartorial passion.

The house in Princeton Walk had a quiet rhythm. Every morning, Vilayat Khan asked Amma for freshly kneaded dough. He would touch it and murmur a prayer: 'Let me never forget that whatever I am doing today is because of you ...' He would then step out on the deck and set the tiny dough balls in a neat row as if he were setting up a langar or feast. He became obsessed with feeding squirrels. The little creatures soon recognised that they had a devoted benefactor in their midst, and bounded in from all over the neighbourhood. Some of them grew fat and lazy and sunbathed on the deck all day. If he forgot to feed them, they would come tapping on the glass window to remind him, and he hurried outside to oblige them. In the evenings, Khansahib would step out for a walk near the lake and offer the same little bits of food to the ducks and geese that glided across the water with upper-class East Coaster poise.

During the summer months, when the air buzzed with an orchestra of insect sound, the deck became the centrepoint of activity. Vilayat Khan could be found there for long hours with just his rosary beads for company. He loved to barbecue, and personally went to the store to pick up different cuts of meat. He liked having people around him, but did not necessarily want to discuss music. Instead, he chatted about cars, politics, food and engineering innovations, going into detail about the heating pipes or cars.

He had many non-musical friends who may have initially started out as students, but gradually grew into a support group in a territory where Vilayat Khan was an immigrant first, maestro second. He, in turn, became a father figure for many of the people who had left behind extended families. He was always 'Abba' and Lisa was 'Amma'.

Weekends were devoted to teen patti, the easy card game that is filled with bluffs and laughter, with a regular gang of friends. Both Abba and Amma had an incredibly competitive streak. By some strange stroke of luck, which no one questioned, one of the two Khans always won. Vilayat Khan was the ultimate bluff-master, able to mesmerise card partners the way he bewitched his audiences. It was almost as if he had some supernatural power to will victory no matter what cards he held. The card games would be followed by a lavish potluck. The gathering would start late afternoon and carry on into the night. There was no drinking, but every so often, Vilayat Khan would step outside to smoke his beedi.

After his stroke, Amma had managed to get her husband off tobacco and alcohol, but beedis remained his little companions till the end. He smoked the Puttu brand, which any visitor arriving from India had standing instructions to carry. He also had smaller custom-made ones acquired from an old contact in Calcutta, which were made with extra saffron and elaichi. Since he enjoyed smoking them till the very end, he had the length reduced so that it was just that little bit less harmful to his lungs, and also so that they would fit into his little silver beedi box.

At one of their gatherings, amma had used disposable plates like most others in America so that she wouldn't have to deal with the washing up. When he saw the styrofoam crockery, he was livid. 'We will eat only off china, no matter how many people there are. This is the home of Vilayat Khan, not some cheap eatery,' he said. Amma and Hidayat looked at each other and did not say a word. She had momentarily forgotten that every object in his life had to be a perfect musical phrase, no matter how inconvenient it might be to others.

His musical life was fairly inactive, and he had very few students at this time. He never took money from students anyway, because he believed that what he was giving them could not be reduced to a transaction. He used to tell them that 'shahgird', which means student, could be broken into 'shah' or king and 'gird' to circle around. That is all he expected—that his students circle around him, the shah.

One of his most beloved students at this time was a young man called Humayun Khan, whose family had listened devotedly to Vilayat Khan's performances in Afghanistan in the 1960s before they escaped to America. He recalled the first time he sat before Abba.

'Get the tanpura.'

Humayun brought it and was giving it to him to tune, when Vilayat Khan said, 'No, son, you tune it.'

Humayun was filled with trepidation and his hand was trembling as he moved the knobs of the instrument around. Right then, he got his first lesson.

'Remember one thing, son. Even if you are a five-year-old child and are sitting in front of great masters, as soon as you have your instrument in hand, you are the ustad. You have to have that level of confidence. And if some day you actually become an ustad and you are listening to a five-year-old child, listen like a student because there will always be something you can learn.'

Another student, Madhu Nanduri, a software engineer by day, recalled that his lessons were never just about music. There would be philosophy and history, and stories about some court musician, and funny moments and just conversation. The music transfer took place when all the conditions were just right—the teacher's mood, the student's mood, the silence around, the colour of the maple tree and the birds outside the window. When Khansahib was sitting on the deck with his rosary beads, the mood would be one of prayer. If the maple tree had turned burnt sienna, then that would colour the tone of the music.

Vilayat Khan still loved going on long drives with no particular destination in mind. When the road forked, he would opt for the scenic route even if it was longer. His life was not constrained by time.

In 1998, fed up with being dependent on others to drive him around, he decided to apply for his American driving licence. He had a friend help him prepare for the written exam and sat like a student, meticulously learning the various road signs. During the driving test, with the evaluator sitting next to him, Vilayat started the car.

'Seat belt, sir,' said the evaluator.

'I always wait for the car to tell me to put it on after I start the engine,' he replied. The evaluator could scarcely know that this candidate had a precision and method in everything he did. Vilayat Khan drove smoothly, elegantly and confidently, and parallel parked perfectly. He immediately qualified.

He fought boredom by continuing to tinker with his cars for hours. After an episode where he was let down by his first love, the Mercedes, he switched allegiances and bought a sleek black BMW 750iL, paying 160,000 dollars in cash. The car brought back a semblance of the old Vilayat Khan—for he had it fitted with bulletproof windows, massaging seats, and a monogram he designed with the initials 'VHK'. The numberplate read: SITAR. But he retained a touch of the old parsimony, and would insist that Hidayat drive out several miles to a gas station that sold cheaper fuel than the one right next to the house.

By this time, there was a vibrant concert circuit across America, especially in the New York–New Jersey area, which was heavily populated with Indians. Vilayat Khan looked forward to the stream of visiting musicians, especially if it included an old friend with whom he had played or partied. When he heard that Hariprasad Chaurasia was performing somewhere in the county, he sent Hidayat to the concert venue with an important message: dine with me. During the interval, Hidayat went backstage to meet the jovial flautist from Bombay.

'Abba insists that you come home for dinner after the

concert. He has spent all afternoon cooking partridge curry for you.'

To Hidayat's surprise and amusement, Chaurasia wrapped up the concert earlier than he was meant to, muttering that he was not feeling too well, and slipped out the back before the concert organisers could stop him. Soon, he was in Hidayat's car, driving towards Princeton Walk, guffawing. At the house, he changed into a chequered lungi and the two musicians ate and laughed late into the night.

In 1996, the World Music Institute hosted a duet with Bismillah Khan and Vilayat Khan at Town Hall in New York. Browning was attempting to recreate a famous recording the two artistes had done together in the early sixties for His Master's Voice. The shehnai master was eighty years old and had come with a big entourage—his sons, a nephew, his grandson who played the tabla, and his manager. They were staying at a hotel in midtown Manhattan. After they arrived and rested for a day, Browning rented a van and drove the whole lot to Princeton.

They rang the bell and Vilayat Khan himself opened the door. When he saw Bismillah Khan standing there with his earring sparkling in the morning sun, his face lit up. They held each other in a long embrace. The two maestros were meeting after a decade at least. Within minutes of greeting and hugging, they had their instruments out and were playing to each other. Later, Amma cooked a delicious lamb curry and they all ate together.

The following evening, their concert was virtually sold out—a 1,400-strong audience sat and listened to the wave after wave of beauty that emerged from the stage. It was as if two lovers were reuniting, playing memories to each other and sharing their life's journeys through music.

When the weather was good, old friends and students like Arvindbhai from Bombay and Jayanta Chatterjee from Calcutta came to Princeton to spend time with Khansahib. They would go out for Chinese or Mexican food or south Indian dosas. Purvi spent a lot of time there and accompanied Khansahib on his shopping excursions, helping him choose textiles and buttons.

Sometime in 2000, the road in front of the house in Princeton Walk was flooded with men in white turbans—they were the Namdharis from Bhaini Sahib accompanying Satguru Jagjit Singh, who had come to visit his beloved. It may have been a strange sight for the neighbours, but by then they knew that a famous musician lived among them, even if they had no idea who he was. Vilayat Khan was delighted to see Jagjit Singh. He had been depressed about a package that had arrived unexpectedly in the mail a few days earlier. It was the American release of a video of Satyajit Ray's film *Jalsaghar* for which he had directed the music. In the credits, the company had erroneously written: Music by Ravi Shankar. It was as if the shadow never went away. He had not spoken about his feelings to anyone, but people around him knew that he was hurt.

One of Khansahib's favourite musicians was the quiet and soft-spoken singer Ulhas Kashalkar, an unassuming man whose personality came through in his music. He was performing at a small venue in New Jersey and Vilayat Khan happened to be there. After the show, he went backstage to meet him.

'Your Sindhura was very good. It is rarely sung these days. How nice it was to hear it. Here, listen to these two other compositions in the raga.' Vilayat Khan sang for him, right there and then, all of it. 'I will be happy if you learn them, you will sing them well.'

Kashalkar could not believe his good fortune. He felt like a lucky beggar who had just been bestowed with gold coins instead of the usual pennies. When he came back to perform the following year, one of Vilayat Khan's students told him that Khansahib would love to teach him some of his special compositions. He spent the next few days in Princeton learning everything he could, especially Sanjh Saravali. Kashalkar is possibly the only person who sings it today.

There were still some bits left to learn, but Kashalkar had to go back to India. A couple of months later, on a train from Calcutta to Bombay, he ran into Vilayat Khan and Lisa sitting in a first-class coupé adjoining his compartment.

'Khansahib! You are on a train?'

'I chose not to fly just to be able to enjoy the scenery and the quiet rhythm of a train journey. How else will I get to see the beauty of this country?'

They hugged each other, and Vilayat invited Kashalkar inside his coupé and finished teaching him the composition. Their musical relationship grew every time Khansahib returned to Calcutta, where Kashalkar was associated with the Sangeet Research Academy. But the real sign of love was when Vilayat Khan cooked for someone. The next time Kashalkar came to Princeton, he conjured up a special dal and a mango salad for his vegetarian guest.

During these years, there was a quiet and uncomplicated reconciliation of sorts with Shujaat, who was on a teaching assignment at the University of California in Los Angeles. Both were older and wiser and had moved on from the pain and betrayal of the early days. Sometimes Vilayat Khan would pick up the phone and call to chat about this and that, unmindful that there was a three-hour time difference and Shujaat may have been fast asleep at the time. And his firstborn indulged him, knowing that these were rare moments.

Khansahib still practised regularly, in his bedroom, facing the wall. He had made a small stand for his sitar, designed in his particular and meticulous way. Even on the days that he didn't play the instrument, he made it a point to tune it.

One day, Natasha Nandini, a young friend who was visiting from London, said, 'Abba, may I come inside and listen?'

'No, darling. For then it would no longer be practice, it would become performance.'

Sometimes great ideas collide and merge inadvertently, because that is the nature of truth and beauty. Princeton had always been famous for its great physicists, and right at that moment, Vilayat Khan had invoked one of the most fascinating theories of quantum physics—that the act of observation affects the object being observed.

Around the time that Vilayat Khan moved to Princeton, I was graduating with a degree in Politics from Princeton University. It is entirely possible that we may have crossed each other at an ice cream store on Nassau Street, but he would have been wearing a shirt, pants and tennis shoes, and I would have assumed that he was one of the many nondescript Indian immigrants of north New Jersey.

Twenty-five years later, I took the New Jersey Transit train from New York to Princeton, feeling emotional. Vilayat Khan could have lived anywhere in the world, but here I was, heading to a place of my youth, a place of his old age. I was going to meet Amma and Hidayat, who still lived there, and to see the places he had loved—the lake with the ducks and the maple tree with leaves that turned vermillion in the Fall and cast a deep red tinge across their house, the colour of raga Sindhura.

Amma was waiting for me with her cat Chico. She had made khichdi that afternoon, and I was grateful for it because it had that distinctly home-cooked deliciousness that no fine dining can satisfy. If one of the translations of love is service, I could see why Vilayat Khan had loved this woman. She was sweet and simple, she loved to cook and feed, and she melted into the surroundings without much fuss, never feeling the need to draw attention to herself.

On my request, she had taken out some of her late husband's personal possessions so I could get a sense of him. There was his small silver box, fashioned like a miniature trunk. It contained his world—a silver cylindrical holder for toothpicks, a mother-of-pearl medicine box, a round box for his rose-flavoured choona and a square one for his beedis. There was another little box that, when opened, turned into a mini-ashtray with a little resting spot for the beedi. There was also the dwarfish pen he had designed to fit into it. The box, with all it held, was a little metaphor for Vilayat Khan, the man.

The other bit of memorabilia she found belonged to Vilayat Khan, the musician. It was a navy blue diary, as old and frail and significant as a wise old grandmother. It was filled with pages and pages of Urdu writing, each one headed by the auspicious 786 sign in Arabic which translated into: Bismillah-ur-Rahman-ur-Rahim. I picked it up and turned the pages gingerly, as if they were delicate parchment or dried moth wings that might crumble, wiping out hundreds of musical secrets and rare compositions. After he died, someone had attempted to read the notations but gave up because they had been so carefully disguised in a cryptic coded language. Only Khansahib knew what he had written. It was his personal safe deposit vault.

In between, on some pages, there were random scrawls in English, in childish handwriting: *A drop of practice is better than an ocean of theories, advice and talk*.

There were phone numbers of concert organisers, or perhaps old girlfriends. One page had notes about his travel, dated 1953:

Reached Peking at 12.15 a.m.
At 3 p.m.: visit Temple of Heaven
At 7.30 p.m.: Banquet at Peace Hotel

I felt I had stepped into a museum of memories. I had encountered little pieces in a tremendous mosaic to help recreate the picture of a Byzantine genius. Amma made Indian-style milky tea and we chatted about this and that—their days in Dehradun where the cock used to crow in raga Pahadi; their time in London; how much he loved her karela-gosht; how Zila's little boy Faizan came and stayed in Princeton and slept between them; his shoe collection, and how he had a dedicated day when a man would come home to polish the 100 pairs he owned ... She was matter of fact in her memories of Vilayat Khan, neither in awe, nor judgemental. Hidayat was her interlocuter, and filled in the gaps when she was not sure of something, or the picture had faded.

I admired a ruby ring on her finger. And therein lay another tale. When he was a young man, Vilayat Khan was driving home alone in his Mercedes after a concert, and passing through the Chambal Valley, an area legendary for dacoits. A group of men stopped the car and asked for all his cash. He said he had nothing except a crate of whisky and his sitar. They were intrigued and asked him to come to their hideout to play his instrument for them. They were so moved by his music that they said, 'This is a Gandharva in our midst,' and instead of taking anything from him, they gave him a ruby ring.

Amma was full of enthusiasm while describing the episode, which her husband must have repeated to people many times over. Hidayat and I winked at each other and smiled. This was such a fantastic story, it was immaterial whether or not it had really happened.

CHAPTER FOURTEEN

Fading Out

Sometime in the late 1990s, Vilayat Khan and Bismillah Khan were once again on stage together at the maroon and velvety Nehru Centre auditorium in Bombay. Shehnai and sitar were engaged in a magnificent musical conversation.

As the tempo picked up, the solitaire on Vilayat Khan's finger flashed like lightning. Suddenly, he stopped mid-phrase and let out a gasp, inaudible to most of the audience but instantly noticed by two students in the front row. Khansahib's hand moved from the stem of his instrument to his chest. He seemed to have difficulty breathing. He lowered the sitar and looked stricken. The music stopped. His students jumped up onto stage. Vilayat gestured to Bismillah Khan to continue playing, and shuffled towards the wings.

He was taken to the nearby Breach Candy Hospital, and the reputed Dr Farokh Udwadia was called to check on him. A little later, feeling better, Khansahib reached for his long black sherwani and started getting dressed, insisting on going back to complete his performance. Feebly protesting, his students turned helplessly to the doctor.

Dr Udwadia peered down his nose at his patient and

spoke in a stentorian voice: 'Vilayat Khan, you are a national treasure, are you not?'

Khansahib laughed.

'As a citizen of India, do I have some rights over our national assets?'

Vilayat Khan nodded.

'In that case, I am not permitting you to go back to the concert. You must rest here.'

And so he did.

The concert was perhaps the first time that Vilayat Khan was unwell in full public view. After that, his health started deteriorating and he was never fully well. He had an open heart surgery in 1998 in New York and finally quit smoking. But by then his lungs had grown irreparably weak.

In 2000, at a concert organised by Spic Macay, an organisation devoted to music education, in the Shankarlal Hall in Modern School, Delhi, he again had to stop midway to rest. An ambulance and a doctor had been kept on call. He returned to the stage to finish his Shyam Kalyan after taking an injection, and said to the audience:

'I can't play the way I used to. But if nothing else, please listen to my intention ...'

In 2000, the Indian government announced Ravi Shankar's Bharat Ratna. The front page of *The Times of India* carried a controversial piece in which Pandit Jasraj, one of India's most highly regarded singers, declared publicly that Vilayat Khan deserved India's principal award over Ravi Shankar.

It's not as if Khansahib did not care. He did. Sometimes he checked how much Ravi Shankar was getting from concert organisers and asked for just a little more. But the rivalry was dramatised by their students and the buzzing bees of the music world rather than the two artistes themselves. Both probably knew deep within that comparison and competition in music was as pointless as comparing two stars in the Milky Way.

The cultural critic Narayana Menon had once said of them: 'To have two sitar players in our midst of the calibre of Ustad Vilayat Khan and Pandit Ravi Shankar is a measure of the vitality of the music scene. We need them both to widen our horizons and enrich our experience. Two Ravi Shankars would not have served the same purpose. Nor two Vilayat Khans. We want the individuality, the equipment, the achievement of each in his own respective field.'

The issue became a talking point in the music world but life went on, and Vilayat Khan continued to play, teach and, even at that age, be a student of music. Neither fame nor the frailty of age stopped him from wanting to learn something new to bewitch his audiences, to bring them closer to him.

When he was about seventy, Khansahib was on his annual winter excursion from Princeton to Calcutta. His loyal friend Jayanta-da arrived at the airport to receive him in his familiar old Ambassador. As they drove to his flat in Hastings, Vilayat Khan turned to his friend.

'Jayanta babu, did you find him?'

'I did, I did,' Jayanta-da said, looking away and squirming at his own lie.

For about a year, Vilayat Khan had been murmuring about a folk song in raga Bhatiyali that he had heard many years ago. He remembered the tune but couldn't recall the words. All he remembered was that there was a boat, a river and a supari tree, and that it was beautiful and mournful. Whenever he spoke to Jayanta-da on the phone from Princeton, he brought it up. Find me that song …

At first, Jayanta-da dismissed it as one of Khansahib's whimsies. But here he was, many months later, and it was the first thing he was asking for. He couldn't procrastinate anymore. When Vilayat Khan wanted something, he made sure he got it. He became obsessed.

In the 1950s, he had been part of an Indian government-sponsored cultural delegation to Russia. As the lights dimmed in the grand Bolshoi Theatre in Moscow, and the Russian sopranos' voices soared divinely, the young Vilayat Khan started worrying about how the Indian performers could match this beauty. That was when one of the delegates, a Bengali folk singer called Nirmalendu Chowdhury, went on stage and sang the startlingly beautiful song that Khansahib was now haunted by.

Like many magical memories that get eroded in the flow of life, the words of the song had gone. What remained was the emotion. Now, so many years later, he wanted to sing the song.

The folk singer had long since died, but his son Utpalendu Chowdhury was singing the same songs. Jayanta-da managed to get in touch with him. He called him that very day and said that Vilayat Khan wanted to meet him. The surprised singer agreed to come across.

The next day, Khansahib asked again about the boatman's song.

'Did you find it? When is he coming?'

'Tomorrow morning to my house.'

'Good.'

The folk singer arrived in the morning. Vilayat spoke to him about the cultural delegation to Moscow and the lovely time he had with his father. Then he got straight to the point. He brought up the boat and the trees and hummed the tune.

'Can you teach it to me?'

Utpalendu looked aghast. 'Sure,' he mumbled.

Utpalendu got up, said he would be back, and disappeared from the room. About twenty minutes later, there was no sign of him. A baffled Jayanta-da went looking for him, wondering what could have happened. He was told by his staff that the visitor had run down the stairs, almost tripping on his dhoti, and slipped out of the main door. He later found out that Utpalendu was so daunted at the thought of teaching a song to such a great maestro that he had simply fled.

But Khansahib was not deterred. He called Utpalendu and reassured him, and this time, he went to the singer's house. By now, the folk singer had gathered himself. Vilayat Khan sat on the floor next to him.

'What are you doing, Khansahib? You can't sit there. Please sit on the couch.'

'No, I am fine here. Today, I am the student and you are the teacher.'

Utpalendu smiled. He shut his eyes and sweetly sang the song for Vilayat Khan. Khansahib smiled as well as he wrote the words on a piece of paper in Urdu.

About a month later, Vilayat Khan was performing at the Ramakrishna Mission outside Calcutta. He announced, 'I want you to hear this folk tune which I had heard Nirmalendu Chowdhury sing many many years ago. It is an ode to all the boatmen who drift along the rivers of Bengal ...'

He sang it beautifully, and the audience found themselves immersed in all the beauty and sadness of their land.

Deepak Raja once wrote of Vilayat Khan: 'He valued the approval of discerning and cultivated audiences, and eschewed populism of every variety. But his was not a snobbish elitism that makes music inaccessible to the majority. His repertoire was dominated by popular ragas and talas and always had a reasonable component of semi-classical music.'

The thing about Vilayat Khan is that he may have been an

ustad, good and proper, but he never stopped being a student. His battery never died—neither did his sense of humour.

Sometime after this, Vilayat was checking in at the British Airways first-class counter at JFK Airport in New York. He was on his way to a concert in Europe. His son Hidayat was accompanying him. The big brown Paxman leather sitar case was taken off the trolley and placed in front of the attendant.

'Sir, what does this contain?'

'It's a sitar,' Khansahib grunted with some irritation. 'An Indian instrument.'

'A seetaaaar!' The British Airways man at the counter suddenly became animated. 'I know Raaaavi Shankar. I love Raaaaavi Shankar. I love what he did with the Beatles. Do you know Raaaaavi Shankar?'

Vilayat Khan scowled at him. He'd been through this ridiculous routine so often and yet it irked him every single time, always triggering a mildly nauseous sensation.

Then, suddenly, he grinned widely and said, 'Of course I know him. Didn't you hear, he died this morning? It's so terribly sad. You'll hear it on the news, I'm sure.'

Hidayat almost choked on his blueberry muffin. He twisted his lips in an effort not to laugh, then spun around so that he could hide his face. He didn't know whether to be shocked or amused or embarassed by his father's unorthodox behaviour. Then it hit him, again. This was Vilayat Khan. Enough said.

In January 2004, Vilayat Khan played his last concert. It was a Sunday morning in Ravindra Natya Mandir in Bombay. He had started raga Todi, and barely built up to komal gandhar when he became breathless. He stopped, told Hidayat to continue playing, and left. In the green room, he was nebulised and given an injection.

Yogesh Samsi was on the tabla. While continuing to play with a heavy heart, he had a flashback to the time Khansahib and he were together a few years back, in a hotel in Calcutta. The night before the concert, Vilayat Khan had placed his sitar on a beautiful carpet next to his bed because he wanted to see it first thing in the morning. Yogesh walked into the room just as Khansahib was waking up and watched him pick it up and play a few notes of Bilaskhani Todi. Only when he was satisfied that the sitar was perfectly in tune did he get on with his day.

He later said to the young tabla player, 'If you really want to play well, you must adore your instrument like a beloved. *Apne saz se khoob mohabbat karo …*' It was a dream within a dream—he had heard this before. Maybe it was his grandfather who had said the same thing to him, for Yogesh's grandfather had learned under Mohammed Khan, Vilayat Khan's brother-in-law. Or did it come from his own teacher, Alla Rakha? These were all great artistes who had shared so many musical and non-musical pearls, often without even saying it. Yogesh knew that some day, somewhere, another musician would inherit this wisdom.

Vilayat Khan came back to the stage and said to the audience, 'I remember leaving you at gandhar, so I will play from there for you.' He played alaap–jod–jhala for another forty-five minutes. After that he played a beautiful Bhairavi, the abiding love of his life.

It was his last concert.

A few weeks later, Vilayat Khan was in Calcutta at Jayanta-da's home in Ballygunj. He was coughing incessantly and had lost his sense of taste. An x-ray had revealed that he had advanced lung cancer. The family had taken a decision not to tell him.

When the doctor left, Vilayat Khan said softly, 'I have been feeling so unwell, you think I have the big C?'

Amma and Hidayat looked away. Jayanta-da said, 'That is not something you have to worry about, Khansahib. You just have to play your sitar.'

Like a child, Vilayat Khan quietly got up and went into his room. He was in his short-sleeved vest and pajamas. He faced the window which overlooked the Birla temple and played raga Gaur Sarang, for it was the middle of the afternoon. A soft, cool breeze blew in. It was the last week of February and Calcutta was just wrapping up its winter. Everyone was sitting behind him, listening, but he was oblivious to their presence.

That was the last time he touched his sitar.

CHAPTER FIFTEEN

Unstruck Sound

The mood outside Jaslok Hospital's intensive care unit is always fraught, but in those first two weeks of March 2004, the emotional intensity was palpable. Inside, on bed #9, lay one of India's greatest musicians, fading in and out of consciousness.

Visitors and well-wishers drifted in. Some came to say goodbye, some to get blessings. They all blended in with the movie playing in his head, and with a score that would go on forever.

He heard the drone of the tanpura, the earthing in his life. He saw the grand old men and women of music float past, and touched their feet one by one while humming their music. He was in Calcutta, inside a stilt house with the Hooghly flowing just outside his window, and the boatman's song wafted high into the sky like a sweet lament. He recognised the familiar comforting scent of his wife. He felt Shujaat's lips kissing his hand. He heard Hidayat's soft voice. He heard himself say, look after each other.

Now he was driving around Shimla and his car floated high above the pine trees. He yearned for something but didn't know what. He heard a voice say 'bhaiya' and felt someone touching his feet lightly. He was running up the dark stairs of a rickety building and he could hear the first call to prayer in raga Bilaskhani Todi and he saw green minarets pierce the blue sky; the scene turned into a palace in Afghanistan and he was facing majestic snow mountains in the distance while a long alaap in raga Darbari made everything emerald green, and then suddenly it was Tilak Kamod in pink and white and blue, and he was laughing with dragonflies and ducks by a lake.

Raga Megh, bold and beguiling, and a dark grey sky. He was walking hand in hand with Amir Khan on Marine Drive in the rain, allowing the waves to drench them, and they saw a blurry Ravi Shankar in the distance and waved at him, laughing joyously. He heard an Urdu poem about flowers and prayer. The music changed to Chandni Kedar and he was ballroom dancing with a beautiful silvery princess in front of the Taj Mahal, and then playing badminton with his daughters while the fountains threw up water in perfect synchronicity. He drifted into the sky and was now floating high above.

He heard raga Basant. Below, through a molten yellow haze, he could see a young boy with a small sitar sitting between a woman with big silver anklets on her feet and a man with long, curly locks, holding a baby on his lap. He ran across the triangular courtyard of the house into the garden at the back. He heard someone lovingly say, Miyan, one day you will be great …

He saw raga Bhairavi floating towards him, in blue and gold, and he heard soft, tinkling laughter. Suddenly, the scale changed. The music grew louder and more thunderously beautiful and finally became deafening as it slowly slipped over him like an invisible comforter. Then there was silence.

Gratitude

Books are never solo operations. This one was made possible by some beloved people who contributed both directly and tangentially.

First, thanks to Hidayat Khan for persuading me to write a book about his father and promising that he would not interfere, even if it made him uncomfortable. Arvind Parikh and Purvi Parikh have always been incredibly generous with their time and knowledge. Deepak Raja, for his insights on the subject and for his time. Thanks to Shujaat Khan for sharing his stories, and Imrat Khansahib for his memories.

Karan and Rati Madan made their New York home available to me so that I could follow Khansahib's footsteps in America. In fact, the idea of the book was born on their balcony! Anju Pratap Singh offered me her lovely home in Mashobra so that I could explore Khansahib's time in Shimla.

My readers who gave me thoughtful feedback include Meera Devidayal, Meenal Baghel, Shanta Gokhale, Bachi Karkaria, Jaishree Goyal, Natasha Nandini, Anisha Agerwala Seth, Mohammed Hanif, Rishi Jindal, Rajni George, Chiki Sarkar, Naheed Carrimjee, Siddharth Pillai and many others.

Thanks to my agent Shruti Debi, my publisher V.K. Karthika and my amazing editor Ajitha G.S., and the entire Westland team. Thank you Rachana Shah for designing the book and Ishika Mohan Motwane for taking the author picture.

Many thanks to the Hamied Foundation for funding this project and enabling me to travel to all the places in which Vilayat Khan lived.

The following books and publications helped me immensely with my research: *Komal Gandhar* by Vilayat Khan (with Shankarlal Bhattacharya, translated by Meena Bannerjee), an extended essay on Vilayat Khan in *Sruti* magazine by Deepak Raja, *The Glorious Tradition of Etawah–Imdadkhani Gharana* by Arvind Parikh, *Networks of Music and History: Vilayat Khan and the Emerging Sitar* by Hans Utter, *Hindustani Music in Colonial India* by Aneesh Pradhan, *Raga Mala* by Ravi Shankar, *The Dawn of Indian Music in the West* by Peter Lavezzoli, *The Gramophone Company's First Indian Recordings* by Michael Kinnear and *Tangled Tapes* by K.S. Mullick.

I have to thank all my family, my unwavering support, especially Chaitanya Motwane, who listened to my endless stories about Vilayat Khan and laughed at the really funny ones, many of which haven't made it into the book.

Finally, thank you, Vilayat Khan, for the music.